THE SHOOTING SCRIPT

JUNO

THE SHOOTING SCRIPT

JUNO

SCREENPLAY AND INTRODUCTION BY DIABLO CODY

FOREWORD BY JASON REITMAN

A Newmarket Shooting Script® Series Book

NEWMARKET PRESS • NEW YORK

FIRST EDITION

10   9   8   7   6   5   4   3

ISBN-13: 978-1-55704-802-8

Library of Congress Catalog-in-Publication Data available upon request.

QUANTITY PURCHASES

Companies, professional groups, clubs, and other organizations may qualify for special terms when ordering quantities
of this title. For information, write to Special Sales, Newmarket Press, 18 East 48th Street, New York, NY 10017;
call (212) 832-3575 or 1-800-669-3903; FAX (212) 832-3629; or e-mail info@newmarketpress.com.

Website: www.newmarketpress.com

Manufactured in the United States of America.

OTHER BOOKS IN THE NEWMARKET SHOOTING SCRIPT® SERIES INCLUDE:

CONTENTS

FOREWORD

BY JASON REITMAN

I was terrified to meet Diablo Cody.

Her name alone is the ultimate intimidator. Add to that the tattoos, the vernacular, and the ever-changing punk rock hair and you can imagine my fear when I was asked to meet her at the bar of the Farmer's Daughter motor lodge. Her pick.

All joking aside, what really scared me was the fear that the voice on the page would not live up to the name. The words wouldn't live up to the woman.

Reading *Juno* is like hearing jazz for the first time. It's your first mouthful of Pop Rocks. The first time you put on 3D glasses. Combinations of words you've never experienced and yet you know their exact meaning. It's exhilarating and joyful. By the end of page 1, you know you've stumbled upon one of those voices that will define a generation. A Tarantino. A Kevin Smith. A Wes Anderson.

I was in the midst of writing my own screenplay when *Juno* landed in my hands. By the time I read the closing lines of Diablo's debut, my own screenplay was officially on hold. *Juno* left me with that feeling in my gut that if I didn't direct it, I would regret that mistake for the rest of my life.

All of this is running through my mind as Diablo orders a dirty martini at the Farmer's Daughter. What followed was a conversation that left me with the rarest of feelings in this industry. Not only is Ms. Cody a delightful drinking partner, but she is the real deal. An authentic voice that brings intelligence and sophisticated wit to complicated real-life situations without ever feeling self-important. She is the voice of cool that we hear in our heads but never can translate through our own pens.

I envy your chance to read these words for the first time.

—November 2007

INTRODUCTION

BY DIABLO CODY

My name is Diablo Cody—well, not really. But who cares? Artifice is typically encouraged in Hollywood, even rewarded. This is a town where our "all-natural" golden girls are (literally) peroxided to the teeth and tanned into non-putrescible leather. A place where sworn enemies swallow their bile and swap "power hugs" on Highland. Even the sky looks like a matte painting on blue-hot afternoons, when the clouds are as firmly set as Jayne Mansfield's hair and the sun blazes immodestly. It's all pretty cool, but it sure as hell ain't real.

That's just one reason why I'm still slack-jawed with shock that *Juno*—a funky little movie that wears its heart on both sleeves—ever came into being. I wrote the script back in Minnesota, a circumstance that should have logically counted as a strike against me. Sometimes I wrote at my kitchen table, sometimes I wrote at the local Target, sometimes I'd sneak a few blocks of dialogue during my precious fifteen-minute breaks at work. *Juno* became my secret passion, and I anticipated our time together like a horny schoolgirl. I don't know if anyone believed that I could actually write a movie, and neither did I. Unlike the moist-browed screenwriters pimping their wares in cruel Burbank, I wrote in a comfortable vacuum.

Ironically, the person who brought this wholly Midwestern script to life was a quintessential Hollywood boy: Jason Reitman. I mean, he's the scion of a friggin' filmmaking dynasty! This is a guy who grew up knowing the Ghostbusters personally (and if you were a kid in the '80s, you know that's fucking rad). And yet, when we first met above a gun shop on Sunset, he radiated a warmth and authenticity that are in short supply out here. He just seemed way too cool—too real—to be an A-list director's son. Put it this way:

I spent my college years watching MTV and leeching off my poor middle-class parents. Meanwhile, Reitman, the so-called "child of privilege," sold ad space in calendars at USC to fund his first short films. His work ethic belies his pedigree.

Reitman and I connected instantly, even though he jokes that he was scared of my tattoos. Frankly, I was scared of his talent. I'd mustered up some confidence in the script by then, but I couldn't have anticipated that someone like Jason—an incredible writer in his own right—would put his own shit on hold to direct *Juno*. But he did, and within months, we were rolling in Vancouver. It was fully ridiculous. There are no words to describe what it's like to watch actors like Ellen Page and Allison Janney breathing life into the inert "blue baby" that is an unproduced screenplay. I'd hang by the monitors for hours, mentally freaking the fuck out. It's hard to say what was more joyful: actually writing *Juno* or surrendering the script to these talented people.

I've written other screenplays since *Juno* and I hope, God willing, that I get to write more. But as Jason has frequently reminded me, you only get one first film. And like Juno MacGuff, who (improbably) finds true love at sixteen, I was fortunate enough to have been "deflowered" cinematically in the nicest possible way. The entire process—from writing, to production, to release—was so warm, so exhilarating, and most of all, so real. In Hollywood, that's rarer than the sashimi at a CAA party.

I hope you all dig reading the script as much as I enjoyed writing it. And here's my unsolicited advice to any aspiring screenwriters who might be reading this: Don't ever agonize about the hordes of other writers who are ostensibly your competition. No one is capable of doing what you do. No one else can ever be you, unless they're some kind of succubus and/or Jodie Foster in *Freaky Friday*. You were born with something that simply cannot be copied, much like a top-secret hand-couriered George Lucas script. Put that in your pretentious little pipe and smoke it.

Thank you,

"Diablo Cody"
November 2007

JUNO

by

Diablo Cody

EXT. CENTENNIAL LANE - DUSK

JUNO MacGUFF stands on a placid street in a nondescript
subdivision, facing the curb. It's FALL. Juno is sixteen years
old, an artfully bedraggled burnout kid. She winces and shields
her eyes from the glare of the sun. The object of her rapt
attention is a battered living room set, abandoned curbside by
its former owners. There is a fetid-looking leather recliner, a
chrome-edged coffee table, and a tasteless latchhooked rug
featuring a roaring tiger.

                         JUNO V.O.
                It started with a chair.

INT. BLEEKER HOUSE - MOLD-O'-RIFFIC BASEMENT- NIGHT

*FLASHBACK - Juno approaches a boy hidden by shadow. He's
sitting in an overstuffed chair. She slowly, clumsily lowers
herself onto his lap.*

A 60's Brazilian track plays from a vintage record player.

                    WHISPERED VOICE
                *Do you know how long I've wanted
                this?*

                    JUNO
                Yeah.

                    WHISPERED VOICE
                Wizard.

EXT. CENTENNIAL LANE - CONTINUED

A DOG barks, jarring Juno back to reality.

                         JUNO
                Quiet, Banana. Hey, shut your gob
                for a second, okay?

We see a teacup poodle tethered in the yard a few feet away
from the abandoned living room set. The dog yaps again.

                         JUNO (V.O.)
                This is the most magnificent discarded
                living room set I've ever seen.

She swigs from an absurdly oversized carton of juice and
wipes her mouth with the back of her hand.

BEGIN ANIMATED TITLE SEQUENCE:

                                                        (CONTINUED)

3   CONTINUED: 3

Juno marching down various street, pumping her arms like a
jogger and chugging intermittently from the huge carton of
juice. We watch her breathlessly navigate suburbia, clearly
on a mission.

4   OMITTED   4

5   OMITTED   5

6   EXT. DRUGSTORE - DAY   6

Finally, a panting Juno arrives at DANCING ELK DRUG on the
main drag of her small Minnesota suburb, Dancing Elk.

The automatic doors of the store part to reveal Juno's
flushed serious face. She carelessly flings the empty juice
container over her shoulder and onto the curb. A group of
DROPOUTS with skateboards near the entrance glare at her.

She enters the DRUGSTORE.

7   INT. DRUGSTORE - CONTINUOUS   7

ROLLO, the eccentric drugstore clerk, sneers at Juno from
behind the counter. He wears a polyester uniform vest.

                    ROLLO
              Well, well. If it isn't MacGuff the
              Crime Dog! Back for another test?

                    JUNO
              I think the last one was defective.
              The plus sign looked more like a
              division sign.

Rollo regards her with intense skepticism.

                    JUNO
              I remain unconvinced.

Rollo pulls the bathroom key out of reach.

                    ROLLO
              This is your third test today, Mama
              Bear. Your eggo is preggo, no doubt
              about it!

An eavesdropping TOUGH GIRL wearing an oversized jacket and
lots of makeup gapes at Juno from the beauty aisle.

                                                      (CONTINUED)

                    TOUGH GIRL
         Three times? Oh girl, you are *way*
         pregnant. It's easy to tell. Is
         your nipples real brown?

A pile of stolen COSMETICS falls out of the girl's jacket and
clatters to the floor.

                    TOUGH GIRL
         Balls!

Juno crosses and crosses her legs awkwardly, hopping. It's
obvious she has to use the bathroom urgently.

                    ROLLO
         Maybe you're having twins. Maybe
         your little boyfriend's got mutant
         sperms and he knocked you up twice!

                    JUNO
         Silencio! I just drank my weight in
         Sunny D. and I have to go, pronto.

Rollo sighs and slips her the bathroom key. Juno races down
one of the aisles.

                    ROLLO
         Well, you know where the lavatory is.
           (Calling after her))
         You pay for that pee stick when
         you're done! Don't think it's yours
         just because you've marked it with
         your urine!

                    JUNO
         Jesus, I didn't say it was.

                    ROLLO
         Well, it's not. You're not a lion
         in a pride!
           (to himself)
         These kids, acting like lions with
         their unplanned pregnancies and
         their Sunny Delights.

8   INT. DRUGSTORE - BATHROOM - DAY   8

In the dim, reeking public bathroom, Juno hovers over the
commode with her boxer shorts around her ankles. She clumsily
tries to use the pregnancy test.

8   CONTINUED: 8

We see the test box sitting on the sink. It's a TeenWave
Discount Pregnancy Test. The accompanying outdated package
photo is of a shrugging 80s teen with a resigned expression.
The fine print on the box reads "From the makers of Sun-Glitz
Lightening Hair Spritz!"

9   INT. DRUGSTORE - FRONT COUNTER - DAY   9

Juno holds the developing test in her hand and slaps the open
test box on the front counter. Rollo scans it and bags it
indifferently.

                         JUNO
              Oh, and this too.

She places a giant licorice Super Rope on the counter.

                         ROLLO
              So what's the prognosis, Fertile
              Myrtle? Minus or plus?

                         JUNO
              (examining stick) I don't know.
              It's not...seasoned yet. Wait. Huh.
              Yeah, there's that pink plus sign
              again. God, it's unholy.

She shakes the stick desperately in an attempt to skew the
results. Shake. Shake. Nothing.

                         ROLLO
              That ain't no Etch-a-Sketch. This
              is one doodle that can't be undid,
              homeskillet.

10   EXT. MACGUFF HOUSE - EVENING   10

Juno walks slowly and dejectedly up the street to her house,
gnawing on the Super Rope. She stops and loops the Super Rope
over a low-hanging tree branch, contemplating how to fashion
a noose.

Juno trudges toward her HOUSE. The yard is a wild tangle of
prairie grass and wild flowers.

11   OMITTED   11

12   OMITTED   12

13   OMITTED   13

14   INT. MACGUFF HOUSE - JUNO'S BEDROOM - NIGHT   14

Juno's BEDROOM is decorated with punk posters: The Damned,
The Germs, the Stooges, Television, Richard Hell, etc.

She picks up a hamburger-shaped phone to call her best
friend, LEAH.

15   OMITTED   15

16   *OMITTED*   16

17   INT. LEAH'S HOUSE - BEDROOM - NIGHT   17

LEAH's room is cluttered with the sentimental junk that
certain girls love to hoard. The PHONE rings.

                    LEAH
               (answering phone)
          Yo-yo-yiggity-yo.

                    JUNO
          I am a suicide risk.

                    LEAH
          Is this Juno?

                    JUNO
          No it's Morgan Freeman. Got any
          bones that need collecting?

                    LEAH
          Only the one in my pants.

                    JUNO
               (in low tones)
          Dude, I'm pregnant.

                    LEAH
          Maybe it's just a food baby. Did
          you have a big lunch?

                    JUNO
          It's not a food baby. I took three
          pregnancy tests today. I am
          definitely up the spout.

                                            (CONTINUED)

17   CONTINUED: 17

                         LEAH
              How did you even generate enough
              pee for three pregnancy tests?

                         JUNO
              I drank like ten tons of Sunny
              Delight. Anyway, yeah. I'm
              pregnant. And you're shockingly
              cavalier.

                         LEAH
              Is this for real? Like *for real,
              for real?*

                         JUNO
              Unfortunately, yes.

                         LEAH
              Oh my God! Oh shit! Phuket
              Thailand!

                         JUNO
              That's the kind of emotion I was
              looking for in the first take.

                         LEAH
              Well, are you going to go to
              Havenbrooke or Women Now for the
              abortion? You need a note from your
              parents for Havenbrooke.

                         JUNO
              I know. Women Now, I guess. The
              commercial says they help women now.

                         LEAH
              Want me to call for you? I called
              for Becky last year.

                         JUNO
              Eh, I'll call them myself. But I do
              need your help with something very
              urgent.

18   EXT. CENTENNIAL LANE - NIGHT   18

        Leah and Juno struggle to drag a recliner across a well-
        manicured suburban lawn. They make a formidable team.

                         LEAH
              Heavy lifting can only help you at
              this point.

                                                            (CONTINUED)

18   CONTINUED: 18

                              JUNO
                    That is sick, man.

Leah busts a gut laughing. It's a stunningly accurate
portrayal of Bleeker's parents.

                              LEAH
                    So, you were bored? Is that how
                    this blessed miracle came to be?

                              JUNO
                    Nah, it was a premeditated act. The
                    sex, I mean, not getting pregnant.

                              LEAH
                    When did you decide you were going
                    to do Bleeker?

                              JUNO
                    Like, a year ago, in Spanish class.

19   *INT. DANCING ELK SCHOOL - SPANISH CLASS - DAY - (FLASHBACK)* 19

*Bleeker and Juno are sitting at their desks, listening to a
teacher lecturing about spanish. Bleeker discreetly pushes a
POSTCARD to Juno with his foot. She picks it up off the
floor, reads it, then looks at Bleeker, who is watching the
teacher obediently.*

20   EXT. CENTENNIAL LANE - NIGHT   20

                              LEAH
                    Aha! You love him.

                              JUNO
                    It's extremely complicated, and I'd
                    rather not talk about it in my
                    fragile state.

She hefts a coffee table with her bare hands. She's wearing
her father's LIFTING BELT.

                              LEAH
                    So, what was it like humping
                    Bleeker's bony bod?

                              JUNO
                    It was magnificent, man!

21   OMITTED   21

22   OMITTED   22

23   OMITTED   23

23A   OMITTED   23A

24   INT. BLEEKER'S BEDROOM - MORNING   24

        CU of Bleeker putting on double socks in his Car-Bed.

        CU of Bleeker putting on his sweat bands.

        CU of Bleeker applying Runner's Glide.

25   INT. KITCHEN - BLEEKER'S HOUSE - KITCHEN - MORNING   25

        CU of a CROISSANT POCKET warming in the microwave.

26   EXT. BLEEKER HOUSE - MORNING   26

        PAUL BLEEKER steps onto the front porch of his house for
        early morning track practice. He wears a cross country
        uniform that reads "DANCING ELK CONDORS." He is eating some
        kind of microwaved snack gimmick.

        Bleeker is startled to discover that Juno is outside waiting
        for him. She has somehow arranged the living room set on the
        front lawn, and is seated in the armchair, chewing a pipe
        officiously.

                        JUNO
                Hey Bleek.

                        BLEEKER
                Hey, cool tiger. Looks proud.

                        JUNO
                Yeah, I swiped it from Ms. Rancick.

                        BLEEKER
                Cool.

                        JUNO
                Your shorts are looking especially
                gold today.

                        BLEEKER
                My mom uses color-safe bleach.

(CONTINUED)

26   CONTINUED: 26

                              JUNO
                    Go Carole.
                         (a beat)
                    So, guess what?

                              BLEEKER
                         (shrugs)
                    I don't know...

                              JUNO
                    I'm pregnant.

Stunned silence. Juno pops up the footrest of the recliner
and leans back comfortably.

                              BLEEKER
                    I guess so.
                         (fidgeting)
                    What are you going to do?

The Dancing Elk Prep cross country team runs past Bleeker's
house in a thundering herd, wearing a motley assortment of
warm-ups. Their momentum stirs the crackling fall leaves.
They wave and holler at Bleeker and Juno.

                              JUNO V.O.
                    When I see them all running like
                    that, with their *things* bouncing
                    around in their shorts, I always
                    picture them naked, even if I don't
                    want to. I have intrusive thoughts
                    all the time.

27   *OMITTED*   27

28   EXT. BLEEKER HOUSE - CONTINUED   28

                              BLEEKER
                    I'm supposed to be running.

                              JUNO
                    I know.

There's an awkward silence.

                              BLEEKER
                    So, what do you think we should
                    do?

> JUNO
> I thought I might, you know, nip it
> in the bud before it gets worse.
> Because I heard in health class that
> pregnancy often results in an infant.

> BLEEKER
> Yeah, typically. That's what
> happens when our moms and teachers
> get pregnant.

> JUNO
> So that's cool with you, then?

> BLEEKER
> Yeah, wizard, I guess. I mean do
> what you think is right.

> JUNO
> I'm real sorry I had sex with you.
> I know it wasn't your idea.

> BLEEKER
> Whose idea was it?

> JUNO
> I'll see you at school, O.K.?

She mounts her bicycle and waves before riding off.

> BLEEKER
> (to nobody in particular)
> Whose idea was it?

29   EXT. DANCING ELK SCHOOL - DAY   29

Juno pushes her crappy bike into the bike rack and winds a
lock around it. In the background, a group of 3 NERDS play a
live-action RPG.

> NERD
> You did not! You don't have the
> armor. That Orc Armor you bought
> from the wizard doesn't have the
> power level to parry my hit!

29A   INT. DANCING ELK SCHOOL - CORRIDOR - DAY   29A

Juno tries to push through the masses, but the throng of
students is thick and unwielding.

30   INT. DANCING ELK SCHOOL - HALLWAY - DAY   30

Juno rummages through her locker, which is plastered with
photos of Leah and Bleeker, plus a giant poster of Iggy Pop
in his heyday.

She grabs a dilapidated physics textbook. A few pages slip
out. STEVE RENDAZO (the same asshole who harassed her as she
walked to the drugstore) passes by in the hallway.

                    STEVE RENDAZO
          Hey, your book fell apart!

                    JUNO
          Yeah.

                    STEVE RENDAZO
          It must have looked at your face.
          PWAH!

He high-fives his klatch of buddies and moves along.

                    JUNO V.O.
          The funny thing is that Steve Rendazo
          secretly wants me. Jocks like him
          always want freaky girls. Girls with
          horn-rimmed glasses and vegan
          footwear and Goth makeup. Girls who
          play the cello and wear Converse All-
          Stars and want to be children's
          librarians when they grow up. Oh
          yeah, jocks eat that shit up.

We see Steve looking back at Juno for a brief second with
mixed feelings.

                    JUNO V.O.
          They just won't admit it, because
          they're supposed to be into perfect
          cheerleaders like Leah. Who,
          incidentally, is into teachers.

We see Leah at the far end of the hallway, talking animatedly
with a paunchy middle-aged teacher, KEITH.

                    LEAH
               (from a distance)
          Me too! I *love* Woody Allen!

31   INT. DANCING ELK SCHOOL - SCIENCE LAB - DAY   31

STUDENTS bustle in, as the teacher, MR. TINKER tries to maintain order. Juno heads toward her desk and sets down her bag.

                    MR. TINKER
          People! We're doing our
          photomagnetism lab today, so find
          your partner and break out into
          fours.

Juno looks up and meets eyes with her longtime lab partner: Bleeker. Sound the gong of awkwardness!

Juno and Bleeker head separately over to an available lab station and unpack their bags in silence.

                    JUNO
          Well! Nothing like experimenting.

                    BLEEKER
          I did the prep questions for this
          lab last night. You can copy my
          answers if you need to.

He slides a piece of graph paper in front of Juno without looking at her.

                    JUNO
          Oh, I couldn't copy your work.

                    BLEEKER
          But you copy my work every week.

                    JUNO
          Oh yeah. I'm kind of a deadbeat lab
          partner, huh?

                    BLEEKER
          I don't mind. You definitely bring
          something to the table.

                    JUNO
          Charisma?

                    BLEEKER
          Or something.

The other two LAB PARTNERS, a humorless couple, join them at the station.

                                        (CONTINUED)

                    JUNO
          So, who's ready for some
          photomagnificence?

                    GIRL LAB PARTNER
          I have a menstrual migraine, and I
          can't look at bright lights today.

                    GUY LAB PARTNER
          Amanda, I told you to go to the
          infirmary and lie down. You never
          listen.

                    GIRL LAB PARTNER
          No Josh, I don't take orders. Not
          from you and not from any man.

                    GUY LAB PARTNER
          You know, you've been acting like
          this ever since I went up to see my
          brother at Mankato. I told you,
          nothing happened!

                    GIRL LAB PARTNER
          Something happened. Because your
          eyes? Are very cold? They're very
          cold, Josh. They're cold, lying eyes.

                    GUY LAB PARTNER
          What? My eyes are not lying!

                    GIRL LAB PARTNER
          Yes they are, Josh. Since Mankato,
          they have been lying eyes.

Juno and Bleeker observe the argument like tennis spectators,
fascinated by the dynamics of a real couple.

                    BLEEKER
          Okay...I'm going to set up the
          apparatus. Juno, want to get a C-
          clamp out of that drawer?

                    GIRL LAB PARTNER
          I'm going to the infirmary.

                    GUY LAB PARTNER
          Good. Call me when you're OFF the
          rag.

> GIRL LAB PARTNER
> Fine. Call me when you learn how to
> love just one person and not cheat
> at your brother's college just
> because you had four Smirnoff Ices
> and a bottle of Snow Peak Peach
> flavored Boone's!

> GUY LAB PARTNER
> Good, I'll be sure to do that,
> Amanda. I'll make a note of it.

He furiously scrawls a fake memo in his notebook.

> JUNO
> Snow Peak Peach *is* the best flavor
> of Boone's. Right, Bleek?

Bleeker reddens and continues constructing the apparatus.

GIRL LAB PARTNER stalks off dramatically.

Bleeker shakes his head and rifles through his textbook.

32   INT. MACGUFF HOUSE - JUNO'S BEDROOM - AFTERNOON   32

Juno examines a large ad in the newspaper that depicts a
distraught TEEN GIRL clutching her head in a moment of staged
conflict. The ad reads: "Pregnant? Find the clinic that gives
women choice. Women's Choice Health Center."

Juno picks up her hamburger phone and dials. For a moment,
she attempts to copy the melodramatic pose from the ad,
checking herself out in the mirror.

> JUNO
> (talking along with voice prompt)
> *"Para instruciones en Espanol,
> oprima numero dos."*

She presses a few buttons in succession.

> JUNO
> Yes, hello, I need to procure a hasty
> abortion?...What was that? I'm sorry,
> I'm on my hamburger phone and it's
> kind of awkward to talk on. It's
> really more of a novelty than a
> functional appliance.

She SMACKS the phone a couple of times.

(CONTINUED)

32   CONTINUED: 32

                              JUNO
                    Better? Okay, good. Yeah, as I said,
                    I need an abortion, two
                    ...sixteen...Um, it was approximately
                    two months and four days ago that I
                    had *the* sex. That's a guestimate.
                    Okay, next Saturday? Great.

She hangs up the phone.

                              JUNO V.O.
                    I hate it when adults use the term
                    "sexually active."

33   *INT. HEALTH CLASS - DAY (FLASHBACK)*   33

A HEALTH TEACHER in slo-mo puts a condom on a banana.

                              JUNO V.O. (CONT'D)
                    What does that even mean? Can I
                    deactivate someday, or is this a
                    permanent state of being? I guess
                    Bleeker went live that night we did
                    it. I guess he hadn't done it before,
                    and that's why he got that look on
                    his face.

34   *INT. BLEEKER'S HOUSE - MOLD-O'-RIFIC BASEMENT - NIGHT*   34
       (FLASHBACK)

*We see Paulie's face at the moment of his deflowering: he's
comically wide-eyed with shock.*

35   INT. MACGUFF HOUSE - DINING ROOM - NIGHT   35

Juno, her father MAC, her stepmother BREN, and LIBERTY BELL
sit at a very typical kitchen table, eating dinner. MAC
shovels food while chatting about his day.

                              MAC
                    You should have seen this octopus
                    furnace. I had to get out my Hazmat
                    suit just to get up in there...

                              JUNO V.O.
                    My dad used to be in the Army, but
                    now he's just your average HVAC
                    specialist. He and my mom got
                    divorced when I was five.
                              (MORE)

                                                          (CONTINUED)

35   CONTINUED: 35
                              JUNO V.O. (cont'd)
                    She lives on a Havasu reservation
                    in Arizona...

        PHOTO: ARIZONA TRAILER PARK

                              JUNO V.O.
                    ... with her new husband and three
                    replacement kids. Oh, and she
                    inexplicably mails me a cactus
                    every Valentine's Day.

36   INT. MACGUFF HOUSE - JUNO'S BEDROOM - DAY   36

        PILE OF NEGLECTED CACTI festering in a corner of Juno's room.

                              JUNO V.O.
                    And I'm like, "Thanks a heap,
                    Coyote Ugly. This cactus-gram
                    stings even worse than your
                    abandonment."

37   INT. MACGUFF HOUSE - DINING ROOM - NIGHT   37

        BREN is cutting up LIBERTY'S food diligently. Her nails are
        brilliant, holding the silverware.

                              JUNO V.O.
                    That's my stepmom, Bren...

        INT. BREN'S WORKROOM - DAY

        Bren stitches a needlepoint pillow of a dog.

                              JUNO V.O.
                    She's obsessed with dogs...

38   EXT. BREN'S TENS - DAY   38

        Bren's nail salon in all its glory.

                              JUNO V.O.
                    ... owns a nail salon called Bren's
                    Tens...

39   INT. BREN'S TENS - DAY   39

        Bren chats up a customer as she applies a fresh coat.

                                                            (CONTINUED)

39   CONTINUED: 39

                         JUNO V.O.
              ... and she always smells like
              methylmethacrylate.

40   INT. MACGUFF HOUSE - DINING ROOM - NIGHT   40

Liberty Bell coughs pitifully as Bren leans over her plate.

                         MAC
              So Juno, how did your maneuver go
              last night?

                         JUNO
              Which maneuver, sir? The one in which
              I moved an entire living room set
              from one lawn to another, or the one
              in which I cleared a sixty-four ounce
              blue slushie in ten minutes?

Bren speaks in her strong city accent.

                         BREN
              Juno? Did you happen to barf in my
              urn? Mac, you know that nice urn by
              the front door, the one I got up in
              Stillwater? I found some weird blue
              shit, I mean stuff, *gunk*, in there
              this morning.

                         JUNO
              I would never barf in your urn,
              Brenda. Maybe L.B. did it.

We see Liberty Bell blithely pouring bacon bits onto her
dinner.

                         MAC
              Liberty Bell, if I see one more
              Baco on that potato, I'm gonna kick
              your monkey ass.

41   EXT. WOMEN'S CHOICE CLINIC - DAY   41

Juno trudges toward the front entrance of the clinic. There
is a lone ABORTION PROTESTER, a teenager of Asian descent
holding a hugely oversized sign that reads "NO BABIES LIKE
MURDERING."

                         LONE PROTESTER
                    (chanting in extremely
                     shy, accented voice))
                         (MORE)

                                                     (CONTINUED)

41   CONTINUED: 41

                         LONE PROTESTER (cont'd)
              All babies want to get borned! All
              babies want to get borned!

Juno recognizes the PROTESTER as a classmate of hers.

                         JUNO
              Uh, hi Su-Chin.

                         SU-CHIN
              Oh, hi Juno. How are you?

                         JUNO
              Good. I'm good.
                   (pause)
              Did you finish that paper for
              Worth's class yet?

                         SU-CHIN
              No, not yet. I tried to work on it
              a little last night, but I'm having
              trouble concentrating.

                         JUNO
              You should try Adderall.

                         SU-CHIN
              No thanks. I'm off pills.

                         JUNO
              Wise move. I know this girl who had a
              huge crazy freakout because she took
              too many behavioral meds at once. She
              took off her clothes and jumped into
              the fountain at Ridgedale Mall and
              she was like, *Blaaaaah!* I'm a kraken
              from the sea!"

                         SU-CHIN
              I heard that was you.

                         JUNO
              Well, it was nice seeing you.

She continues on toward the clinic entrance.

                         SU-CHIN
                   (calling out)
              Juno!

Juno stops in her tracks but doesn't bother to turn around.

                                                        (CONTINUED)

> SU-CHIN
>
> Your baby probably has a beating
> heart, you know. It can feel pain.
> And it has fingernails.

> JUNO
>
> Really? Fingernails?

She considers the concept, then pushes open the clinic door.

42   INT. WOMEN'S CHOICE CLINIC - RECEPTION - DAY   42

The receptionist sits behind a pane of bulletproof glass. The
waiting room is semi-crowded, occupied mostly by pregnant
women, teens and ill-behaved children.

> PUNK RECEPTIONIST
>
> Welcome to Women's Choice, where
> women are trusted friends. Please
> put your hands where I can see them
> and surrender any bombs.

Juno flashes her best jazz hands.

> JUNO
>
> Hi. I'm here for the big show?

> PUNK RECEPTIONIST
>
> Your name, please?

> JUNO
>
> Juno MacGuff.

The receptionist raises a pierced eyebrow and arranges some
paperwork on a clipboard.

> JUNO V.O.
>
> She thinks I'm using a fake name.
> Like Gene Simmons or Mother Teresa.

The receptionist hands Juno the clipboard and a pen.

> PUNK RECEPTIONIST
>
> I need you to fill these out, both
> sides. And don't skip the hairy
> details. We need to know about
> every score and every sore.

The receptionist reaches into one of those ubiquitous women's
clinic CONDOM JARS, and holds up a fistful of purple rubbers.

                    PUNK RECEPTIONIST
          Would you like some free condoms?
          They're boysenberry.

                    JUNO
          No thank you. I'm off sex.

                    PUNK RECEPTIONIST
          My partner uses these every time we
          have intercourse. They make his
          balls smell like pie.

                    JUNO
          Congrats.

She takes a seat in the WAITING ROOM and rifles through a
pile of old magazines. The magazine selection is lots of
"mommy mags" and health related periodicals. She selects an
issue of *Family Digest* and gingerly flips through for a few
moments.

Then she looks over and notices the FINGERNAILS of a nearby
teen, who looks as nervous as she does. The girl bites her
thumbnail and spits it onto the floor.

Juno looks away, but immediately notices another waiting
woman, who absently scratches her arm with long fake nails.

Suddenly, she sees fingernails EVERYWHERE. The receptionist
clicks her nails on the front desk. Another woman blows on
her fresh manicure. Everyone seems to be fidgeting with their
fingers somehow. Juno suddenly looks terror-stricken...

                                             CUT TO:

                    PUNK RECEPTIONIST
          Excuse me, Miss MacGoof?

There's no answer. We see that Juno's chair is EMPTY.

The receptionist cranes her neck and sees the front door
drift shut. Juno's figure recedes into the distance as she
tears off down the street, running as fast as she can.

43   EXT. LEAH'S HOUSE - DAY   43

Leah's front door swings open to reveal a breathless Juno
standing sheepishly on the porch. Leah sighs.

> LEAH
>
> What are you doing here, dumbass? I
> thought I was supposed to pick you
> up at four.

> JUNO
>
> I couldn't do it, Leah! It smelled
> like a dentist in there. They had
> these really horrible magazines,
> with, like, spritz cookie recipes and
> bad fiction and water stains, like
> someone read them in the tub. And the
> receptionist tried to give me these
> weird condoms that looked like grape
> suckers, and she told me about her
> boyfriend's pie balls, and Su-Chin
> Kuah was there, and she told me the
> baby had fingernails. Fingernails!

> LEAH
>
> Oh, gruesome. I wonder if the
> baby's claws could scratch your vag
> on the way out?

> JUNO
>
> I'm staying pregnant, Le.

> LEAH
>
> Keep your voice down dude, my mom's
> around here somewhere. She doesn't
> know we're sexually active.

> JUNO
>
> What does that even mean? Anyway, I
> got to thinking on the way over. I
> was thinking maybe I could give the
> baby to somebody who actually likes
> that kind of thing. You know, like
> a woman with a bum ovary or
> something. Or some nice lesbos.

> LEAH
>
> But then you'll get huge. Your chest
> is going to *milktate*. And you have to
> tell everyone you're pregnant.

> JUNO
>
> I know. Maybe they'll canonize me
> for being so selfless.

                         LEAH
            Maybe they'll totally shit and be
            super mad at you and not let you
            graduate or go to Cabo San Lucas
            for spring break.

                         JUNO
            Bleeker and I were going to go to
            Gettysburg for spring break.

Leah sighs, as if there's no helping her nerdy friend.

                         LEAH
            Well, maybe you could look at one
            of those adoption ads. I see them
            all the time in the Penny Saver.

                         JUNO
            There are *ads*? For parents?

                         LEAH
            Oh yeah! "Desperately Seeking
            Spawn." They're right by the ads
            for like, iguanas and terriers and
            used fitness equipment. It's
            totally legit.

                         JUNO
            Come on, Leah. I can't scope out
            wannabe parents in the Penny Saver!
            That's tacky. That's like buying
            clothes at the Pump n' Munch.

44   EXT. PARK BENCH - DAY   44

Juno and Leah are sitting at a bench in a park. They slurp
giant blue slushies and sift through a pile of Penny Savers.
Juno has her pipe with her.

                         JUNO
            The Penny Saver sucks.

                         LEAH
            Yeah, but it sucks for free.

They turn the pages in silence for a moment. Their lips and
teeth are Windex-blue.

                         LEAH
            Look at this one "Wholesome,
            spiritually wealthy couple have
            found true love with each other."
                         (MORE)

                         LEAH (cont'd)
                    (checks to see that Juno
                     is paying attention)
               "All that's missing is your
               bastard."

                         JUNO
                    (reading a different page)
               There's a guy in here who's giving
               away a piano. Free for the hauling!
               We should put it in Bleeker's yard.

                         LEAH
               You're not listening to me.

                         JUNO
               No, I heard you. I just can't give
               the baby to people who describe
               themselves as "wholesome." I'm
               looking for something a little
               edgier.

                         LEAH
               What did you have in mind, a family
               of disturbed loners who are into
               gunplay and incest?

                         JUNO
               I was thinking a graphic designer,
               mid-thirties, and his cool Asian
               wife who dresses awesome and plays
               bass. But I'm trying to not be too
               particular.

                         LEAH
               All right, how about this one?
               "Healthy, educated couple seeking
               infant to join our family of five.
               You will be compensated. Help us
               complete the circle of love."

                         JUNO
               Yeesh, they sound like a cult.
               Besides, they're greedy bitches.
               They already have three kids!

                         LEAH
               Hey, Juno. Juno! Look at this one.

She points to the paper and motions for Juno to look. Juno
scans the ad silently.

44   CONTINUED: (2)   44

We see the ad. It contains a photo of an attractive couple
with ambiguous Mona Lisa smiles. It reads "Educated,
successful couple wishes to..."

                    JUNO V.O.
          They were Mark and Vanessa Loring,
          and they were beautiful even in
          black and white.

45   EXT. BLEEKER HOUSE - PAULIE'S WINDOW - NIGHT   45

We see Paulie's bedroom window-- festooned with childish
curtains-- and the light on inside.

46   INT. BLEEKER'S HOUSE - PAULIE'S BEDROOM - NIGHT   46

Bleeker lies on his Car-bed in his track uniform, listening
to the same LP from when he and Juno went all the way.

He stares between the pages of his embossed Dancing Elk Prep
yearbook.

We see the object of his gaze is Juno's black and white
YEARBOOK PHOTO. Next to it, we see a sloppy, handwritten
message from Juno. We hear Juno's voice reading the message:

                    JUNO V.O.
          Hey Bleeker! Spank off to this with
          motion lotion. Just kidding (kind
          of.) Your best friend, Juno.

Bleeker picks up the phone. It's the same HAMBURGER PHONE
Juno has. He reconsiders and puts it down.

There's a knock on the bedroom door.

BLEEKER'S MOM pokes her dowdy head inside.

                    BLEEKER'S MOM
          Paul? Are you coming downstairs to
          eat?

                    BLEEKER
          I don't think so.

                    BLEEKER'S MOM
          You ran eight miles today, Puppy.

                    BLEEKER
          I'm not hungry, oddly.

                                              (CONTINUED)

> BLEEKER'S MOM
> But it's breakfast for supper. Your
> favorite, Paulie. I made French
> toast and sausage. Patties, not
> linkies, just like you like it.

Bleeker places his hand silently on his stomach.

> BLEEKER'S MOM
> Juno MacGuff called while you were
> out running. She wants to know if
> you're coming to her little
> coffeehouse performance on Saturday.

> BLEEKER
> Thanks for the message.

> BLEEKER'S MOM
> You know how I feel about her.

> BLEEKER
> You've mentioned it about fifty
> times.

> BLEEKER'S MOM
> I just hope you don't consider her
> a close friend.

Bleeker's mom gives up and closes the door.

We see that Bleeker is clutching a pair of PANTIES in one
hand, which he slowly releases as the 45 ends.

47   INT. MACGUFF HOUSE - LIVING ROOM - AFTERNOON   47

Bren and MAC are seated on the couch. Leah is standing nearby
for reinforcements. Juno paces nervously, trying to suss out
how to break the massive news.

> JUNO
> I have no idea how to spit this
> out.

> BREN
> Hon, did you get expelled?

> JUNO
> No. The school would probably
> contact you in the event of my
> expulsion.

>   BREN
>   Well, I was just asking. It seemed
>   plausible.

>   MAC
>   Do you need a large sum of money?
>   Legal counsel?

>   JUNO
>   No, no, I'm definitely not asking
>   for anything. Except maybe mercy.
>   Like, it would be really great if
>   nobody hit me.

>   MAC
>   What have you done, Junebug? Did
>   you hit someone with the Previa?

>   LEAH
>   Best to just tell them, man. Rip
>   off the Band-Aid and let it bleed.

>   JUNO
>   I'm pregnant.

Bren and Mac are predictably speechless.

>   BREN
>   Oh, God...

>   JUNO
>   But I'm going to give it up for
>   adoption. I already found the perfect
>   people.

Leah presents the Penny Saver photos of the Lornings.

>   JUNO (CONT'D)
>   They say they're going to pay my
>   medical expenses and everything. I
>   promise this will all be resolved
>   in thirty-odd weeks, and we can
>   pretend it never happened.

>   MAC
>   You're pregnant?

                         JUNO
          I'm so sorry, you guys. If it's any
          consolation, I have heartburn
          that's like, radiating down to my
          kneecaps and I haven't gone number
          two since Wednesday. Morning!

                         BREN
                    (interrupting)
          I didn't even know you were
          sexually active!

Juno cringes upon hearing her most-hated term.

                         MAC
          Who is the kid?

                         JUNO
          The baby? I don't know anything
          about it yet. I only know it's got
          fingernails, allegedly.

                         BREN
          Nails? Really?

                         MAC
          No, I mean the father! Who's the
          father, Juno?

                         JUNO
          Oh. It's, well, it's Paulie
          Bleeker.

Bren and Mac burst into shocked laughter.

                         JUNO
          What?

                         MAC
          Paulie Bleeker? I didn't know he
          had it in him!

                         BREN
                    (giggling)
          He just doesn't look, well, virile.

                         LEAH
          I know, right?

                         MAC
          Okay, this is no laughing matter.

>   JUNO
>   (indignant)
>   No, it's not. Paulie *is* virile, by
>   the way. He was very good
>   in...chair.

Leah fires a *be quiet* glance at Juno.

>   MAC
>   Did you say you were thinking about
>   adoption?

>   JUNO
>   Yeah, well, there's this couple
>   who've been trying to have a baby for
>   five years.

>   LEAH
>   We found them in the Penny Saver by
>   the exotic birds section.

Bren looks understandably alarmed. Juno hastily attempts to
make the situation sound more legitimate.

>   JUNO
>   But they have a real lawyer and
>   everything. I'm going to meet with
>   them next weekend.

>   BREN
>   Junebug, that is a tough, tough
>   thing to do. Probably tougher than
>   you can understand right now.

>   JUNO
>   Well, I'm not ready to be a mom.

>   MAC
>   Damn skippy, you're not! You don't
>   even remember to give Liberty Bell
>   her breathing meds.

>   JUNO
>   Once! And she didn't die, if you
>   recall!

>   BREN
>   Honey, had you considered, you
>   know, the alternative?

Leah and Juno exchange glances.

                         JUNO
          No.

                         BREN
          Well, you're a brave young lady.
          You're made of stronger stuff than
          I thought. You're a little Viking!

                         JUNO
          Cool it.

                         BREN
          First things first, we have to get
          you healthy. You need prenatal
          vitamins. Incidentally, they'll do
          incredible things for your nails, so
          that's a plus. Oh, and we need to
          schedule a doctor's appointment. Find
          out where you're going to deliver.

                         JUNO
          The term "deliver" is so weird. Can
          we not say "deliver"?

                         LEAH
          How does "crap it out" sound?

                         MAC
          Juno, I want to come with you to
          meet these adoption people. You're
          just a kid. I don't want you to get
          ripped off by a couple of baby-
          starved wingnuts.

                         JUNO
          Sure, Dad.

Mac nods, satisfied, then contemplates the situation
dismally.

                         MAC
          I thought you were the kind of girl
          who knew when to say when.

                         JUNO
          I have no idea what kind of girl I
          am.

                         BREN
                (sensing tension)
          Why don't you girls go upstairs for
          a while? I think Mac's gonna blow.

(CONTINUED)

Juno and Leah hightail it upstairs.

>   MAC
>   Just tell it to me straight, Bren.
>   Do you think this is my fault? Her
>   mother's fault?

>   BREN
>   I think kids get bored and have
>   intercourse. And I think Junebug
>   was a dummy about it. But we have
>   to move on from here and help her
>   figure it out.

>   MAC
>   I'm not ready to be a Pop-Pop.

>   BREN
>   You're not going to be a Pop-Pop.
>   And Juno's not going to be a ma.
>   Somebody else is going to find a
>   precious blessing from Jesus in
>   this garbage dump of a situation. I
>   friggin' hope.

>   MAC
>   (conspiratorially)
>   Did you see it coming when she sat
>   us down here?

>   BREN
>   Oh God yeah. But I was hoping she
>   was expelled or into hard drugs.

>   MAC
>   That was my first instinct too. Or
>   D.W.I. Anything but this. And I'm
>   going to punch that Bleeker kid in
>   the weiner the next time I see him.

>   BREN
>   Oh Mac, no! He's a sweet kid. You
>   know it wasn't his idea.

Mac shrugs in agreement.

48   OMITTED   48

48A   OMITTED   48A

49   INT. LORING HOUSE - DAY   49

Music plays as we see SPARSE IMAGES OF VANESSA LORING'S HANDS preparing the house for Juno's arrival -

Sprucing a vase of FLOWERS.

Straightening a FRAMED PHOTO of the Lorings.

Dusting off a table with one of those WETNAPS for furniture.

Lining up a shelf of BOOKS.

50   EXT. LORING NEIGHBORHOOD - PREVIA - DAY   50

The Previa cruises slowly into the Loring's fancy gated community. Mac pulls over and parks on the curb.

51   EXT. LORING HOUSE - FRONT PORCH - DAY   51

Mark and Vanessa Loring have an impressive, though generic McMansion. The entire yard is unlandscaped soil. Mac presses the doorbell while Juno chews her nails uncomfortably. Both look mortified as they wait for someone to greet them.

VANESSA opens the door. She's a pretty, meticulous woman in her early thirties. Very Banana Republic.

                    VANESSA
          Hi! I'm Vanessa. You must be Juno
          and Mr. MacGuff. I'm Vanessa.

                    JUNO
          Vanessa, right?

                    MAC
          Hello. Thank you for having me and
          my irresponsible child over to your
          home.

                    VANESSA
          Oh no. Thank you. Come on in.

52   INT. LORING HOUSE - HALLWAY - DAY   52

Vanessa awkwardly leads them into her home.

                    VANESSA
          Can I take your coats?

                                              (CONTINUED)

                              JUNO
                    Sure.

She takes off her hooded sweatshirt and thrusts it into
Vanessa's arms who sets it on a bench.

                              JUNO
                    Wicked pic in the Penny Saver, by
                    the way. Super classy. Not like
                    those other people with the fake
                    woods in the background. Like I'm
                    really going to fall for that, you
                    know?

                              VANESSA
                    You found us in the *Penny Saver*?

MARK LORING appears next to Vanessa. He's a boyishly
attractive guy in his mid-thirties.

He glances sheepishly at Vanessa upon hearing the Penny Saver
mention, then extends his hand to Mac and Juno.

                              MARK
                    Hi. I'm Mark Loring. I'm the husband.

53   INT.   LORING HOUSE - LIVING ROOM - DAY   53

Mark and Vanessa usher Juno and Mac into the austere,
spacious living room. A woman in a business suit sits on the
couch with a briefcase in her lap.

                              MARK
                    This is our attorney, Gerta Rauss.

                              JUNO
                         (in exaggerated, growling
                          German accent))
                    Geeeerta Rauuuss!

                              GERTA
                         (straight)
                    Nice to meet you.

Mac seizes Mark's hand and pumps it heartily.

                              MAC
                    I'm Mac MacGuff, and this, of
                    course, is my daughter Juno.

                              MARK
                    Like the city in Alaska?

                                                          (CONTINUED)

                         JUNO
               No.

                         MARK
               Cool. Well, let's sit down and get
               to know each other a bit.

                         VANESSA
               I'll get drinks. What would everyone
               like? I've got Pellegrino, Vitamin
               Water...

                         JUNO
               A Maker's Mark, please. Up.

                         MAC
               She's joking. Junebug has a
               wonderful sense of humor, which is
               just one of her many genetic gifts.

                         JUNO
               I also have good teeth. No
               cavities. We finally got
               fluoridated water in Dancing Elk.

She bares them frighteningly to demonstrate.

Vanessa stares, unflappable.

                         MAC
               We're fine, thank you.

Mac and Juno join Mark and Gerta Rauss on the couch.

                         GERTA
               So, Juno. First off, how far along
               are you?

                         JUNO
               I'm a junior.

                         GERTA
               No, I mean in your pregnancy.

                         JUNO
               Oh. Uh, my stepmom took me to the
               doctor yesterday and they said I
               was twelve weeks.

Vanessa enters with the refreshments om a tray.

                    VANESSA
          Oh, that's marvelous. So you're
          almost into your second trimester,
          then?

                    JUNO
          Yeah, apparently. I'm having it on May 4.

                    VANESSA
          The tough part's almost over for you. I
          mean, my girlfriends always tell me the
          first couple months are the hardest.

                    JUNO
          Yeah, but I hardly noticed it. I'm
          more worried about the part where I
          have to start wearing jeans with an
          elastic panel in the front.

                    VANESSA
          I think pregnancy is beautiful.

                    JUNO
          Well, you're lucky it's not you.

Vanessa's looks to the ceiling.

                    MARK
             (clearing throat)
          So, let's discuss how we're gonna
          do this...thing.

                    JUNO
          Well, I just have the baby and give
          it to you, right?

                    GERTA
          Mark and Vanessa are willing to
          negotiate an open adoption.

                    MAC
             (protective)
          Wait. What does that mean?

                    GERTA
          It means they'd send annual
          updates, photos, let Juno know how
          the baby is doing as he or she
          grows up. Of course, Juno's legal
          rights would be terminated...

                         JUNO
            Whoah. I don't want to see pictures.
            I don't need to be notified of
            anything. Can't we just kick it old
            school? I could just put the baby in
            a basket and send it your way. You
            know, like Moses in the reeds.

                         MARK
            Technically, that would be kickin'
            it Old Testament.

Mark and Juno lock eyes.

                         JUNO
            Yeah. Yeah! The way people used to
            do it. Quick and dirty, like
            ripping off a Band-Aid.

                         GERTA
            Well, then we agree a traditional
            closed adoption would be best for
            all involved, then?

                         JUNO
            Shit, yeah. Close it up.

Vanessa is clearly ecstatic.

                         MARK
            Obviously, we'll compensate you for
            your medical expenses.

                         VANESSA
            Are you looking for any other
            compensation?

                         MAC
            Excuse me?

                         JUNO
            Well, no...I'm not going to *sell*
            the baby. I just want it to grow up
            with people who are ready to love
            it and be parents. I'm in high
            school, dude. I'm ill-equipped.

                         VANESSA
            You're doing an amazing and
            selfless thing for us.

                                        (CONTINUED)

> MARK
> Vanessa has wanted a baby since we
> got married.

> VANESSA
> I want to be a mommy so badly!

Juno and Mac stare at her.

> MAC
> You don't say.

> VANESSA
> Well, haven't you ever felt like
> you were born to do something?

> MAC
> Yes. Heating and air conditioning.

> VANESSA
> Well, I was born to be a mother.
> Some of us are.

> JUNO
> Mark, are you looking forward to
> being a dad?

Mark is caught off guard.

> MARK
> Sure, why not? I mean, every guy
> wants to be a father. Coach soccer,
> help with science projects and...I
> don't know. Fatherly stuff.

Mac casts a subtle, dubious glance at Mark.

> VANESSA
> Well, shall we start looking over
> the paperwork? Gerta has already
> drafted some preliminary documents.

> JUNO
> Can I use the facilities first?
> Being pregnant makes you pee like
> Seabiscuit.

> VANESSA
> Sure. The powder room down here is
> being re-tiled, but you can use the
> master bath upstairs. Go up, then
> turn left and on your right...

53   CONTINUED: (5)   53

                              JUNO
                    Room with a toilet, got it.

54   INT. LORING HOUSE - ENTRY/STAIRS - DAY   54

        Juno heads into the foyer and up the stairs. We see a posed
        photo of Mark and Vanessa in the stairwell. Their house is
        beautiful, but frigid. Juno rubs her arms, shivering.

55   INT. LORING HOUSE - BATHROOM - DAY   55

        The Loring's bathroom is huge. Juno flushes and goes to the
        double sink to wash her hands. She opens the overhead
        cabinet and sees Vanessa's toiletries. She spritzes on some
        perfume and examines the more expensive grooming items.
        There's a crinkled tube of LUBE in the cabinet. Juno picks
        it up, fascinated. She rubs a drop of it between her hands
        and runs it through her hair like pomade.

56   INT. LORING HOUSE - UPSTAIRS HALLWAY - DAY   56

        Juno opens the bathroom door and instantly BUMPS into Mark.

                              JUNO
                    Whoops! Yikes, I didn't expect to
                    see you up here.

                              MARK
                    Sorry. I was just getting
                    something.

                              JUNO
                    Did your wife send you up here to
                    spy on me?

                              MARK
                    What? No! Do we come off like
                    paranoid yuppies or something?

                              JUNO
                    Well, you don't just invite a random
                    pregnant teenager into your house and
                    leave her unsupervised. I could be a
                    total klepto, for all you know.

                              MARK
                    I don't get a klepto vibe from you.
                    Evil genius? Maybe. Arsonist?
                    Wouldn't rule it out.

                         JUNO
            I did steal a squirt of perfume. What
            do you think? It's Clinique Happy.

She holds her WRIST up to Mark's twitching nostrils.

                         JUNO (CONT'D)
            Smell those sparkling topnotes!

Mark inhales.

                         MARK
            Am I supposed to feel happy now?

                         JUNO
            You should be happy, Holmes. I'm
            giving you and Vanessa the gift of
            life. Sweet, screaming, pooping
            life! And you don't even have to be
            there when the baby comes out of me
            all covered in...

                         MARK
            Viscera?

                         JUNO
            Blood and guts.

                         MARK
            We'd better get back downstairs ASAP.

Juno mocks his use of "ASAP" silently.

                         JUNO
                    (halting)
            Wait a minute. Is that a Les Paul?

Juno is staring into a room with the door slightly ajar. We
see GUITARS mounted on the wall, and the edges of posters.

                         MARK
            Oh. That's, uh, my room. Vanessa lets
            me have a room for all my old stuff.

                         JUNO
            Wow, you get a whole room in your
            own house? She's got you on a long
            leash there, Mark.

                         MARK
            Shut up.

57   INT. LORING HOUSE - MARK'S "SPECIAL" ROOM - DAY   57

The walls are plastered with FRAMED POSTERS of early-90s alt
rock bands. (Mudhoney, Jane's Addiction etc.) Mark removes
his LES PAUL from its moorings and hands it to Juno.

                    JUNO
          It's beautiful. I've always liked
          Gibson better than Fender.

                    MARK
          What do you play?

                    JUNO
          I rock a Harmony.

                    MARK
              (holding back a chuckle)
          Oh.

                    JUNO
          What? I'm a pawn shop rocker.

                    MARK
          Sorry. I swear I'm not a gear snob.

Juno turns the guitar over, examining it closely.

                    JUNO
          What is that, Mahogany? What
          happens if you crack the neck?

                    MARK
          Tell me about it. I used to play in
          a really tight band back when I
          lived in Chicago, and one night we
          opened for the Melvins...do you
          know who the Melvins are?

                    JUNO
              (lying)
          Yeah.

                    MARK
          Well, we were playing with them and I
          busted this guitar onstage. It cost me
          $800 and a dime bag just to have it fixed.

                    JUNO
          When was this, like '96?

                                          (CONTINUED)

> MARK
> '93. I'm telling you that was the
> best time for rock and roll.

> JUNO
> Nuh-uh, 1977! Punk Volume 1.
> You weren't there, so you can't
> understand the magic.

> MARK
> You weren't even alive!

58   INT. LORING HOUSE - LIVING ROOM - DAY   58

Vanessa, Mac and Gerta Rauss are waiting in awkward silence
for Juno and Mark to return. Mac notices a brand new PILATES
MACHINE sitting in its packaging in a corner of the room.

> MAC
> So. What's that thing?

> VANESSA
> A Pilates machine?

> MAC
> What do you make with that?

> VANESSA
> You don't *make* anything. It's for
> exercising.

58A   INT. LORING HOUSE - MARK'S SPECIAL ROOM - SAME   58A

Mark and Juno tool around on the guitars unplugged. They play
little riffs. He teaches her a couple chords.

58B   INT. LORING HOUSE - LIVING ROOM - SAME   58B

> MAC
> My wife just ordered one of those Tony
> Little Gazelles off the TV, you know,
> from the guy with the ponytail?

Vanessa and Gerta have no response.

> MAC
> That guy just doesn't look right to me.

58B   CONTINUED: 58B

Suddenly, a shriek of AMP FEEDBACK, followed by loud,
discordant GUITAR STRUMMING can be heard drifting down from
upstairs. Vanessa's looks to the ceiling.

                    VANESSA
                (to her guests)
            Will you excuse me?

59   INT. LORING HOUSE - MARK'S SPECIAL ROOM - DAY   59

Mark has strapped on the Les Paul and is playing and singing.
"Doll Parts" by Hole.

                    JUNO AND MARK
                (quietly singing together)
            "Yeah, they really want you... they
            really want you... they really do."

Building together.

                    JUNO AND MARK
                (singing together and
                 connecting)
            Yeah, they really want you... they
            really want you... and I do to.
                (both blush)

VANESSA appears in the doorway. Juno immediately puts down
the guitar. Mark doesn't notice her immediately.

                    MARK
                (passionate singing)
            I WANT TO BE THE...
                (notices Vanessa)
            Oh, sorry honey...

Mark clumsily puts down the guitar and stands up.

                    VANESSA
            You guys are *playing music*?

                    MARK
            Juno just wanted a closer look at
            Kimber here.

                    JUNO
            Your guitar is named *Kimber*?

                    MARK
            Yeah.

                                          (CONTINUED)

>   JUNO
> That's all right. My axe is named
> Roosevelt. After Franklin, not Ted.
> Franklin was the hot one with the
> polio.

>   VANESSA
> I think Gerta is waiting for us
> downstairs with some important
> stuff for us to go over.

Mark hangs the guitars back on the wall. He and Juno exit the
room, chastised. Vanessa looks to Mark in question.

>   VANESSA
> Didn't mean to interrupt the jam
> sessions.

60   INT. LORING HOUSE - ENTRY - DAY   60

Juno and Mac have put their coats on and are in the process
of leaving. Gerta hands Juno the DOCUMENTS. Vanessa and Mark
trail behind.

>   GERTA
> So, look those over and give me a
> call at my office if you have any
> questions.

>   VANESSA
> Juno, we'd really appreciate it if
> you could keep us updated on any
> doctor's appointments, ultrasounds,
> other things of that nature.

>   JUNO
> Oh. Sure. Of course you'd want to
> know how your kid is cooking.

>   VANESSA
> So, then, you really think you're
> going to go ahead with this?

Mac STARES at Juno gravely.

>   JUNO
> Yeah. For sure. I like you guys.

Juno looks at Mark.

> VANESSA
> How sure? Percentage-wise, would
> you say you're 80% sure, 90% sure?

Mark seems visibly embarrassed by Vanessa's manic demeanor.

> JUNO
> I'm going to say I'm 104% sure.

> VANESSA
> Oh really?

> JUNO
> Look, if I could give it to you now,
> I would. But it probably looks like a
> Sea Monkey at this point, so I think
> we should leave it in there for a
> while until it gets cuter, you know?

> MAC
> I think that's a great idea.

> MARK
> That's great, right? Stellar news.
> Well, you guys drive safe, and we'll
> hear from you soon, all right?

> MAC
> All right, take care of yourselves.

Juno and Mac exit. Mark shuts the door. All is silent in the
foyer. Mark, Vanessa and Gerta stand motionless. Gerta pumps her
fist triumphantly, trying to create a mood of celebration.

> GERTA
> (overly aggressive)
> All RIGHT!

Vanessa buries her head in her hands and weeps hoarsely.

61   EXT. SUBURBAN STREETS - MORNING   61

It is now WINTER. The TRACK TEAM jogs in formation, leaving
tracks in the snow. Those bastards never stop running.

62   EXT. DANCING ELK SCHOOL - TRACK - DAY   62

Bleeker is running alone on the track. His exhalations are icy
puffs in the air. Bleeker's friend VIJAY jogs up alongside him.
Vijay is a solemn, skinny boy, much like Bleeker.

62   CONTINUED: 62

                         VIJAY
               Hey man.

                         BLEEKER
               Oh, hey Vijay.

                         VIJAY
               Did you hear Juno MacGuff is
               pregnant?

                         BLEEKER
               Yup.

                         VIJAY
               Just like our moms and teachers!

                         BLEEKER
               Yup.

                         VIJAY
               Did you hear it's yours?

                         BLEEKER
               Yup.

                         VIJAY
               What a trip, man.

                         BLEEKER
               I don't really know anything about it.

                         VIJAY
               You should grow a moustache. You're
               a real man now.

                         BLEEKER
               I can't grow a moustache. It never
               comes in evenly.

                         VIJAY
               Me neither. But I'm going to stop
               wearing underpants in order to
               raise my sperm count. See you.

VIJAY jogs off. Bleeker STOPS and wipes away his sweat.

62A   INT. DANCING ELK SCHOOL - HEAD OFFICE - DAY   62A

We're looking over Juno's now FIVE MONTH PREGNANT BELLY to a
school administrator filling out a slip.

Juno takes the slip, turns around and smiles all the way out.

62B   INT. DANCING ELK SCHOOL - CORRIDOR - DAY   62B

Juno exits the head office and bumps into Bleeker.

                    BLEEKER
          Hey Juno... A couple of us are
          going to the cineplex after school
          to donut that movie with the guy
          with eighteen kids.

                    JUNO
          Sorry, Bleek... Going for my
          ultrasound. Gotta note and
          everything.

                    BLEEKER
          Okay, cool.

                    JUNO
          I'll try to drop by later.

63   INT. DOCTOR'S OFFICE - AFTERNOON   63

SPLOOGE! We see ultrasound goo being squirted onto Juno's
exposed pregnant belly. An ULTRASOUND TECHNICIAN is using a
Doppler device to view the contents of her burgeoning bump.
Bren and Leah *ooh* and *ahh* at the resulting image.

The tech takes measurements and types them into her database.

                    ULTRASOUND TECH
          That's the feet...

                    ALL THREE
          Oooh...

                    ULTRASOUND TECH
          And there's a hand...

The monitor reveals the baby's head.

                    ALL THREE
               (various)
          Check that out... No way...

                    BREN
               (dreamily)
          Would you look at that?

                    LEAH
          Check out Baby Big-Head. That kid
          is *scary!*

                                        (CONTINUED)

                         JUNO
           Hey, I'm a *sacred vessel*. All you've
           got in your belly is Taco Bell!

                         LEAH
           Touche.

                         JUNO
               (gazing at the monitor)
           It *is* really weird looking. It's
           like it's not even real. I can't
           believe there are saps who actually
           cry at these things.

Juno and Leah look at BREN, who is dabbing her eyes
discreetly.

                         BREN
           What? I'm not made of stone.

                         ULTRASOUND TECH
           Well, there we have it. Would you
           like to know the sex?

                         LEAH
           Aw, please Junebug?

                         JUNO
           No way. No, I definitely don't want
           to know.

                         ULTRASOUND TECH
           Planning to be surprised when you
           deliver?

                         JUNO
           I want Mark and Vanessa to be
           surprised, and if I know, I won't
           be able to keep myself from telling
           them and ruining the whole thing.

                         ULTRASOUND TECH
               (condescending)
           Are Mark and Vanessa your friends
           at school?

                         JUNO
           No, they're the people who are
           adopting the baby.

                         ULTRASOUND TECH
           Oh. Well, thank goodness for that.

                         BREN
          Wait, what's that supposed to mean?

                    ULTRASOUND TECH
          I just see a lot of teenage mothers
          come through here. It's obviously a
          poisonous environment for a baby to
          be raised in.

Juno, Leah and Bren become immediately defensive.

                         JUNO
          How do you know I'm so poisonous?
          Like, what if the adoptive parents
          turn out to be evil molesters?

                         LEAH
          Or stage parents!

                         BREN
          They could be utterly negligent.
          Maybe they'll do a far shittier job
          of raising a kid than my dumbass
          stepdaughter ever would. Have you
          considered that?

                    ULTRASOUND TECH
          No...I guess not.

                         BREN
          What is your job title, exactly?

                    ULTRASOUND TECH
          Excuse me?

                         BREN
          I said, what-is-your-job-title,
          Missy?

                    ULTRASOUND TECH
          I'm an ultrasound technician, ma'am.

                         BREN
          Well I'm a nail technician, and I
          think we both ought to stick to
          what we know.

                    ULTRASOUND TECH
          What are you talking about?

63   CONTINUED: (3)   63

                              BREN
                    You think you're special because
                    you get to play Picture Pages up
                    there?

Bren gestures to the ULTRASOUND MONITOR.

                              BREN
                    My five year-old daughter could do
                    that, and let me tell you, she is not
                    the brightest bulb in the tanning
                    bed. So why don't you go back to
                    night school in Manteno and learn a
                    real trade!

The ULTRASOUND TECH exits in a huff.

                              JUNO
                    Bren, you're a dick! I love it.

64   INT. JUNO'S BEDROOM - DAY   64

Juno lays in bed checking out the ULTRASOUND PRINT OUT.

65   EXT. LORING NEIGHBORHOOD - PREVIA - AFTERNOON   65

The Previa drives into the front gate of Mark and Vanessa's
exclusive community. A sign on the gate reads "Glacial
Valley."

66   EXT. LORING HOUSE - ENTRY - AFTERNOON   66

Juno rings the doorbell, shifting her weight in the cold.

MARK answers the door, dressed in a t-shirt and jeans.

                              MARK
                    Juno? Wow, I didn't expect to see
                    you here.

                              JUNO
                    I've got something really cool to
                    show you guys. Is Vanessa here?

                              MARK
                    No, she's working late tonight.
                    She's trying to accrue some extra
                    time off for when, you know...

He gestures awkwardly to Juno's belly.

                                                        (CONTINUED)

66   CONTINUED: 66

                         JUNO
                    Right. I hear they can be kind of a
                    time-suck.

                         MARK
                    Come on in. You wanna Ginseng Cooler?

                         JUNO
                    Sure. What is it with you rich
                    people and your herb-infused
                    juices?

                         MARK
                    I don't know. Something to do with
                    the four-packs...
                         (adding)
                    ... They're not bad.

67   INT. LORING HOUSE - KITCHEN - AFTERNOON   67

       Mark leads Juno into the kitchen, where he pours two drinks.
       The STEREO blares in the background.

                         JUNO
                    Why aren't you at work?

                         MARK
                    I mostly work from home. I'm a
                    composer.

                         JUNO
                    No shit. Like Johannes Brahms?

                         MARK
                    No, more commercial stuff.

                         JUNO
                    Like what?

                         MARK
                    Commercials.

                         JUNO
                    Oh.

                         MARK
                    Have you seen those ads for
                    Titanium Power men's deodorant?

> JUNO
> (singing)
> Titanium Power! Get more snatch by
> the batch!

> MARK
> I wrote that.

> JUNO
> You're kind of a sellout, aren't
> you? What would the Melvins say?

> MARK
> They'd say you came a long way out here
> not knowing if anyone would be home.

She holds up a manila envelope.

> JUNO
> Come on, you're going to want to
> sit down for this.

68   INT. LORING HOUSE - DEN - AFTERNOON   68

As they move into the living room, Juno sits down and motions
for Mark to join her on the couch.

> JUNO
> Park it, dude.

Mark sits down. With great fanfare, Juno retrieves a dark,
glossy sheet from the envelope. It's her ULTRASOUND.

> JUNO
> Behold, good sir! The very first
> photo of your future child.

> MARK
> You're kidding!

Mark EXAMINES the ultrasound, baffled.

> JUNO
> I think it kind of looks like my
> friend, Paulie.

> MARK
> (joking)
> Oh, is <u>he</u> bald and amorphous?

> JUNO
> No, he's the dad.

Mark looks jolted, as if it's the first time he considered
that her baby might have a father. He stands up and holds the
photo up to the light critically.

                    MARK
          Can you tell if it's a boy or a
          girl?

                    JUNO
          The doctor can tell, but I decided
          not to know. I want it to be a big
          surprise.

                    MARK
          Well, it can really only go two ways.

                    JUNO
          That's what you think. I drink tons
          of booze so you might get one of
          those scary neuter-babies that's
          born without junk.

                    MARK
          Junk?

                    JUNO
          You know... it's parts...

                    MARK
          I know what junk is.

                    JUNO
               (teasing)
          Yeah?

                    MARK
          We definitely want it to have junk.

                    JUNO
          Well don't worry about it. My
          stepmom is forcing me to eat really
          healthy. She won't even let me
          stand in front of the microwave or
          eat red M&Ms. Hope you're ready.

Mark chuckles.

                    MARK
          Wait...do you hear that?

A new SONG has begun. Mark closes his eyes in ecstasy and
walks toward the stereo. Juno follows him toward the source
of the music, looking perplexed by how happy he is.

> JUNO
> What is it?

> MARK
> It's only my favorite song. It's
> Sonic Youth doing "Superstar" by
> the Carpenters.

> JUNO
> (excited)
> I've heard the Carpenters before.
> Chick drummer and freaky dude. Not
> unlike the White Stripes.

> MARK
> You haven't heard the Carpenters
> like this. Listen.

Mark grabs the STEREO REMOTE off the kitchen counter and
turns up the volume to a roar. Mark and Juno stand in silence
in the kitchen. Mark mouths along with the lyrics.

> MARK
> (lipsynching)
> *Don't you remember you told me you*
> *loved me, baby...*

> JUNO
> Hey, I like this.

> MARK
> This album is all Carpenters covers
> by alt-rock bands. It's called *If I*
> *Were a Carpenter*. It is God. I'll
> rip a copy for you before you
> leave.

> JUNO
> You don't have to do that.

> MARK
> It's the least I can do. What did
> you say your favorite band was?

> JUNO
> I didn't. But it's a three-way tie
> between the Stooges, Patti Smith
> and the Runaways.

> MARK
> Yeah, I definitely need to make you
> some CDs. At least while my kid is
> hanging out in there.

He gestures at Juno's burgeoning paunch.

Mark walks over to his music collections and starts pulling CD's. He's got a Carpenter's disc, the "No Alternative" charity compilation, and Mother Love Bone.

Juno spots a VHS TAPE on the coffee table and picks it up.

> JUNO
> (reading title)
> *The Wizard of Gore?*

> MARK
> (distracted)
> Oh yeah. It's Herschel Gordon Lewis.
> He's the ultimate master of horror.

> JUNO
> Please. Dario Argento is the ultimate
> master of horror.

Mark SWIVELS AROUND slowly on his desk chair, surprised.

> MARK
> Argento's good, but Lewis is
> completely dimented. We're talking
> buckets of goo. Red corn syrup
> everywhere. And fake brains up the
> yin-yang.

> JUNO
> (examining the tape box)
> Frankly, this looks kind of stupid.

Mark gives a look - "Oh, Really?"

69   INT. LORING HOUSE - DEN - AFTERNOON   69

We see some particularly memorable footage from *The Wizard of Gore.*

Mark and Juno are watching the movie and drinking root beer floats. They're sitting dangerously close on the sofa.

> JUNO
> (watching movie)
> This is even better than *Suspiria.*
> You've got decent taste in slasher
> movies, Mark.

                              MARK
                    Here's to dovetailing interests.

He raises his mug in a toast and Juno clinks it awkwardly.

                              JUNO
                    So, have you and Vanessa thought of
                    a name for the baby yet?

                              MARK
                    Well, sort of. Vanessa likes
                    Madison for a girl.

                              JUNO
                         (aghast)
                    Madison? Isn't that kind of...I
                    don't know, gay?

                              MARK
                    God, pretentious much? I guess
                    everyone should have a mysterious
                    name like Juno, huh?

                              JUNO
                    My dad went through this phase
                    where he was obsessed with Greek
                    and Roman mythology. He named me
                    after Zeus's wife. I mean, Zeus had
                    other lays, but I'm pretty sure
                    Juno was his only wife. She was
                    supposed to be really beautiful but
                    really mean. Like Diana Ross.

                              MARK
                    That suits you.

                              JUNO
                    Uh, thanks.

                              MARK
                    You know, not many teenage girls in
                    your situation would actually go
                    through with this.

                              JUNO
                    I weighed my options. But after all
                    this, I'm glad I didn't, you know,
                    get rid of it. I want to have it.
                    For you guys.

                              MARK
                    You're something else.

(CONTINUED)

A door suddenly slams upstairs. Vanessa's home.

>   MARK
>   Vanessa. Shit, you better get out
>   of here.

>   JUNO
>   Why? What the big deal?

>   MARK
>   Nothing. She just hates when I sit
>   around watching movies and 'not
>   contributing.'

>   JUNO
>   I'll handle this. I'm really good
>   at diffusing mom-type rage.

Juno jumps up and rushes out.

>   MARK
>   Wait...aww, crap!

70   INT. LORING HOUSE - KITCHEN - AFTERNOON   70

Vanessa slides her BRIEFCASE off her shoulder and ventures
into the living room. She's struggling to carry some
oversized shopping bags.

>   VANESSA
>   Mark? Are you home? I want to show
>   you some things I picked up.

Juno intercepts her breathlessly, clutching the ULTRASOUND
photo. Mark trails behind her.

>   JUNO
>   Hi Vanessa!

Vanessa JUMPS and makes a strangled sound.

>   VANESSA
>   Juno! God, you startled me. What
>   are you doing here? What's wrong?

>   JUNO
>   Nothing...

>   VANESSA
>   Then what's going on?

                    JUNO
          I went to the doctor today.

Vanessa is obviously entertaining some worse-case scenarios.
Her eyes are wide and she's uncharacteristically ruffled.

                    VANESSA
          Is the baby okay?

                    JUNO
          Sure. It's the right size and
          everything. I even saw its
          phalanges today! Check this...

She holds the ULTRASOUND up to show Vanessa and drapes her
arm around her.

                    VANESSA
          What...

                    JUNO
          This is the baby. Your baby.

Vanessa drops the shopping bags, sick with relief.

                    VANESSA
          Oh my God...

                    JUNO
               (kindly)
          Doesn't it look like it's waving?
          It's kind of like it's saying "Hi,
          Vanessa. Will you be my mommy?"

                    VANESSA
          Yeah. Yeah, it kind of does.

                    MARK
          Juno was nice enough to bring this
          by for us.

                    JUNO
          I came over as soon as I got that
          cold ultrasound goo off my pelvis.
          My stepmom verbally abused the
          ultrasound tech so we were escorted
          off the premises.

                    VANESSA
               (distracted)
          Oh, that's great!

She can't divert her gaze from the photo.

                    JUNO
          See? Nothing to worry about.

Vanessa chuckles tightly, clearly embarrassed by her show of
emotion.

70A   INT. LORING HOUSE - ENTRY WAY - DAY   70A

Vanessa and Mark walk Juno out. Juno peers at some shopping
bags from various kids stores.

                    JUNO
          Hey, what kind of swag did you
          score?

                    MARK
          Yeah. Mall madness, huh?

                    VANESSA
          Oh it's just some stuff I picked
          up. For, you know, the baby.

                    VANESSA
          Babies need a lot of things. I want
          everything to be just right.

                    JUNO
          I thought people got all that stuff
          at baby showers. When my stepmom had
          my sister I remember she got about a
          million presents. They were all lame
          though, so I wasn't jealous.

                    MARK
          I doubt anyone's throwing us a shower.

                    JUNO
          Why?

                    VANESSA
          Um, I think people are kind of
          unsure about the situation because
          it's not, you know, set in stone.

                    JUNO
          What do you mean? You
          mean...(aghast) Do you think I'm
          going to *flake out* on you?

70A   CONTINUED: 70A

> VANESSA
> No, no, I don't think that, Juno.
> It's just that, we went through a
> situation before where it didn't
> work out.

Juno glances at Mark and again at Vanessa. Vanessa looks
embarrassed.

> MARK
> Cold feet.

> JUNO
> You should have gone to China. I heard
> they give away babies like free iPods.
> They shoot 'em out of those T-shirt
> guns at sports events.

> VANESSA
> (abruptly)
> Right. Well, Juno, your parents
> must be wondering where you are.
> You might want to head home.

> JUNO
> Naah. I'm already pregnant, so they
> figure nothing worse could happen
> to me. I gotta bounce anyway. It
> was nice seeing you guys again.

She waves and heads for the door.

> MARK
> (to Juno)
> Hey, don't forget your bag.

Vanessa looks pain-stricken as Mark helps Juno with her bag.

77   EXT. MACGUFF HOUSE - NIGHT   77

Juno kicks the snow off her shoes before she enters.

INT. MACGUFF HOUSE - KITCHEN - NIGHT

Bren sits at the kitchen table with a mug of coffee and an
issue of *Dog Fancy*.

Juno enters nonchalantly, drinking a giant slushie.

CONTINUED:

                    BREN
          Where the hell have you been,
          Junebug?

                    JUNO
          I drove to St. Cloud to show Mark
          and Vanessa the ultrasound. And I
          wound up staying for a couple of
          hours.

                    BREN
          A couple of hours? Why are you
          going up there in the first place?

                    JUNO
          They said they wanted to know about
          this stuff. They said to keep them
          updated, so I did!

                    BREN
          You could have sent it to them. Why
          would you drive an hour out to East
          Jesus, Nowhere?

                    JUNO
          I don't know, I just did. And while
          we were waiting for Vanessa, Mark
          and I watched *The Wizard of Gore*
          and he burned me some CDs of weird
          music. He's kind of cool.

A beat as Bren absorbs this.

                    BREN
          That was a mistake, Juno. Mark is a
          married stranger. You overstepped a
          boundary.

                    JUNO
          Listen, Bren-*duhhh*, I think you're
          the one overstepping boundaries.
          You're acting like you're the one
          who has to go through this and get
          huge and push a baby out of your
          vag for someone else. Besides, who
          cares if he's married? I can have
          friends who are married.

                    BREN
          It doesn't work that way, kiddo.
          You don't know squat about the
          dynamics of marriage.

                                        (CONTINUED)

CONTINUED: (2)

                    JUNO
          You don't know anything about me!

                    BREN
          I know enough.

Bren rises to leave, clutching the *Dog Fancy* magazine.

                    JUNO
          (gesturing to the magazine)
          We don't even have a dog!

                    BREN
          Yeah, because *you're* allergic to
          their saliva. I've made a lot of
          sacrifices for you, Juno. And in a
          couple years you're going to move
          out--and I'm getting Weimaraners.

                    JUNO
          Wow, dream big!

                    BREN
          Oh, go fly a kite.

Bren STORMS out. Juno heads to the URN by the door and
defiantly pours the remains of her blue slushie into it.

71   EXT. BLEEKER HOUSE - NIGHT   71

Juno parks her PREVIA on the street. She walks up to the
house and rings the doorbell.

BLEEKER'S MOM answers, visibly annoyed. Her eyes drift down
to Juno's middle.

                    JUNO V.O.
          Bleeker's mom was possibly attractive
          once. But now she looks a hobbit. The
          fat one that was in *The Goonies.*

                    BLEEKER'S MOM
          Hi Juno. What can I do for you?

                    JUNO
          I borrowed Paulie's physics notes
          in school today. I'm pretty sure he
          needs them back, or his grade could
          plummet to an A minus.

                    BLEEKER'S MOM
          Fine. Come in.

                                              (CONTINUED)

71   CONTINUED: 71

She steals another glance at Juno's belly.

72   INT. BLEEKER HOUSE - HALLWAY - NIGHT   72

Bleeker's mom escorts Juno wordlessly up the stairs and down
the hallway to Paulie's bedroom. Juno discreetly tries to
charge ahead of her, but her expanding middle prevents her
from getting past Bleeker's mom. They share an extremely
awkward moment wedged side-by-side in the narrow hallway.

Bleeker's mom nudges past Juno and knocks on Bleeker's
bedroom door. The door has a cheesy racecar-themed decoration
hanging on it that says *PAULIE'S VRROOOM!* It looks like
something a 5-year old might have.

73   INT. BLEEKER HOUSE - PAULIE'S BEDROOM - NIGHT   73

Paulie is on the floor surrounded by old quizzes, studying
like the tortured brainiac he is. Mrs. Bleeker opens the
bedroom door. Juno appears. Paulie jumps, startled.

                    JUNO
          Hey, don't concentrate so hard,
          man. I think I smell hair burning.

Bleeker smiles faintly.

                    BLEEKER'S MOM
          Ten minutes.

She closes the door halfway and leaves. Juno rolls her eyes
and pulls the door shut entirely.

                    BLEEKER
          What's up?

                    JUNO
          I just wanted to come over. You
          know, say hi. I miss hanging out
          with you on school nights.

                    BLEEKER
          I miss it too.

He nervously cracks open a container of ORANGE TIC-TACS and
pours them into his mouth.

                    JUNO V.O.
          Orange Tic-Tacs are Bleeker's one
          and only vice.
                    (MORE)

73   CONTINUED: 73
                              JUNO V.O. (cont'd)
                    When we made out, the day I got
                    pregnant, his mouth tasted really
                    tangy and delicious.

74   INT. BLEEKER HOUSE - "MOLD-O'-RIFFIC" BASEMENT - NIGHT   74

            CU ON BLEEKER'S MOUTH AS HE KISSES JUNO FOR THE FIRST TIME

75   INT. BLEEKER HOUSE - PAULIE'S BEDROOM - NIGHT   75

            Bleeker glances at Juno's midsection, embarrassed.

                              BLEEKER
                    So, it looks like you're getting
                    pregnant-er these days.

                              JUNO
                    Yeah. Um, I hooked up a whole
                    private adoption thing. These
                    married people in Saint Cloud are
                    going to be the parents.

            Bleeker is visibly relieved.

                              BLEEKER
                    Really? What are they like?

                              JUNO
                    The guy is super cool! His name is
                    Mark and he's into old horror
                    movies and he plays guitar. I
                    actually hung out with him today.

                              BLEEKER
                    Is that normal?

                              JUNO
                    I asked my dad and Bren not to narc
                    us out to your folks, so we should
                    be safe.

                              BLEEKER
                    Oh. That's a relief.

            Juno walks over to the bed and sits down next to Bleeker.

                              JUNO
                    I'm going to really start looking
                    like a dork soon. Will you still
                    think I'm cute if I'm huge?

                                                            (CONTINUED)

> BLEEKER
> I always think you're cute. I think
> you're beautiful.

Juno is caught off guard by his sincerity.

> JUNO
> Jesus, Bleek.

> BLEEKER
> Well, I do.

The song playing ends, and another one begins. It's "the
song," the track that Bleeker and Juno both recognize from
the infamous night in the basement.

> BLEEKER
> Hey Junebug, when all this is over
> we should get the band back
> together again.

> JUNO
> Yeah. Sure. Once Tino gets a new
> drumhead we should be good to go.

> BLEEKER
> We could get back together too.

> JUNO
> Were *we* together?

Bleeker picks at the carpet, dejected.

> BLEEKER
> Well, we were once. You know, that time.

> JUNO
> What about Katrina De Voort? You
> could go out with Katrina De Voort.

> BLEEKER
> I don't like Katrina.

> JUNO
> I totally heard you did.

> BLEEKER
> I don't. Katrina smells like soup.
> Her whole house smells of soup.

76   OMITTED

79   EXT. LORING HOUSE - DAY   79

The house is covered in fresh snow.

80   OMITTED   80

81   INT. LORING HOUSE - NURSERY - DAY   81

Mark and Vanessa stand silently in the nursery. The walls are
primed slate gray. A single ANTIQUE ROCKING CHAIR sits in the
corner. Vanessa beams proudly and holds two paint samples up
near the wall.

                    VANESSA
          What do you think? Custard or
          Cheesecake?

                    MARK
          They're yellow.

                    VANESSA
          Well, I wanted to pick something
          gender-neutral for now. Once we get
          the baby, God willing, we can
          create a more decisive palette.

                    MARK
          Why do people think yellow is
          gender-neutral? I don't know one
          man with a yellow bedroom.

                    VANESSA
          I think I'm leaning toward Custard
          in this light. I don't know. I
          should paint a small area...

                    MARK
          Or you could just wait a couple
          months. It's not like the baby's
          going to storm in here any second
          and demand dessert-colored walls.

                    VANESSA
          What to Expect says that readying the
          baby's room is an important process
          for women. It's called "nesting."

                    MARK
          Nesting, huh? Are you planning to
          build the crib out of twigs and
          saliva?

                                            (CONTINUED)

> VANESSA
> You should read the book. I even
> flagged the "daddy chapters" for you.

> MARK
> I just think it's too early to
> paint. That's my opinion.

> VANESSA
> And I disagree.

Mark shrugs, resigned.

Vanessa points to the nursery's largest wall.

> VANESSA
> That wall is going to need
> something. Maybe we could put our
> first family picture there.

> MARK
> Hm.

> VANESSA
> Can you see it?

Mark stares at the wall, looking lost.

82   OMITTED   82

83   INT. RIDGEDALE MALL - DAY   83

Juno and Leah are walking through the mall, looking bored. Juno
is wearing one of Mac's giant hockey jerseys in lieu of actual
maternity wear. Leah gnaws on a giant cinnamon pretzel.

> LEAH
> Yum. This pretzel tastes like a
> friggin' *donut*!

> JUNO
> Share the love, Tits!

She wrestles Leah for the pretzel. Onlookers stare at them,
appalled, as Leah puts Juno in a half-Nelson.

> JUNO
> (to eavesdroppers)
> She's assaulting me! She's denying
> me fresh-baked goodness!

Leah claps a hand over Juno's mouth.

                    JUNO
               (muffled)
          Hly shht!

                    LEAH
          What?

Juno drags Leah behind a pillar and peers out from behind it.
They're watching a group of well-heeled women and their
children shopping en masse. One of the women is pushing a
toddler in an ultramodern stroller. And one of the women is
VANESSA, looking vaguely detached.

                    JUNO
               (hushed)
          That's her. That's Vanessa Loring.

                    LEAH
          Of the *Penny Saver* Lorings?

Juno nods.

                    LEAH
          No way! She's pretty.

                    JUNO
          You sound shocked or something.

                    LEAH
          I just thought she'd look really
          old in real life.

The women gather near a play area, sip Frapps and loudly
discuss their outfits for an upcoming party.

                    WOMAN #1
          And I was like, "No offense,
          sweetie, but nobody looks good in
          gauchos."

                    WOMAN #2
          Especially not with her build.

                    JUNO
               (mimicking the women,
                Peanuts-style)
          Wah-wah-waaah!

One of the little girls in the group tugs at Vanessa's
sleeve. Vanessa happily follows the little girl over to their
play area and begins to play energetically with her.

                                        (CONTINUED)

Juno watches intently, but Leah just snickers.

> LEAH
> She's gonna steal that kid for her
> collection.

> JUNO
> Right, seriously.

They watch Vanessa for a few more moments. The other kids
wander over toward the play area while their mothers ignore
them. Vanessa continues to entertain the children.

> LEAH
> Bo-ring!

Leah stands up. Juno lingers for a moment.

84   INT. RIDGEDALE MALL - ELEVATOR BANK - A HALF HOUR LATER   84

Leah and Juno approach the elevator.

> JUNO
> I want a huge cookie. And like, a
> lamb kebob. Simultaneously.

> LEAH
> God, Spermy. Must you always feed?

The elevator door opens, revealing... Vanessa.

> VANESSA
> Juno?

Juno tries her best to look enthused.

> JUNO
> Well *hi* Vanessa! What brings you to
> the mall today?

> VANESSA
> Just, you know, shopping with my
> girlfriends.

> LEAH
> You're gay?

Juno glares at Leah.

> VANESSA
> (confused)
> No...

                              JUNO
                    Please excuse Leah. She's mentally
                    challenged.

                              VANESSA
                    Oh, okay. So...how are you feeling?

                              JUNO
                    Happy? Oh, you mean like,
                    physically. I'm good. Look, I have
                    a snooze button now!

She lifts her shirt and presses her popped-out NAVEL.

                              VANESSA
                    That's great.

Vanessa is admiring the belly, when Juno grimaces.

                              JUNO
                    Dude, it's moshing all over.

Vanessa looks confused.

                              JUNO (CONT'D)
                         (explains)
                    It's kicking.

Vanessa nods in understanding then begins summoning the
courage for an unusual request.

                              VANESSA
                    Um... Juno, can I - Can I touch it?

                              JUNO
                    Are you kidding? Everyone at school
                    is always grabbing at my belly. I'm
                    like a legend. They call me the
                    Cautionary Whale.

She grabs Vanessa's hand and plants it on her stomach.

                              VANESSA
                    I can't feel anything.

Vanessa moves her hand, wanting desperately to feel the baby.

                              VANESSA
                    It's not moving for me.

She says this as though it's an admission of failure.

Ellen Page as Juno MacGuff and Michael Cera as Paulie Bleeker

All photos by Doane Gregory

Ellen Page as Juno

Michael Cera as Paulie

Ellen Page as Juno, talking to Leah on her hamburger–shaped phone

Director Jason Reitman directing Ellen Page

From left: Jennifer Garner as Vanessa, looking at the ultrasound test with Ellen Page as Juno

From left: Ellen Page as Juno and Olivia Thirlby as Leah, eating lunch at the Dancing Elk School

From top: Allison Janney as Bren, Ellen Page as Juno, and J.K. Simmons as Mac, rushing off to the hospital

Director Jason Reitman on the set

Writer Diablo Cody on the set

84   CONTINUED: (2)   84

                              JUNO
                    Oh, you should try talking to it.
                    They can apparently hear speech in
                    there, even though it sounds all ten
                    thousands leagues under the sea.

Vanessa kneels down next to the swell of Juno's belly.

                              VANESSA
                    Hi. Hi, baby. It's me. My name is
                    Vanessa. I can't wait to meet you.

Leah gives a look to Juno as if she's about to barf.

                              VANESSA (CONT'D)
                    Can you hear me sweet angel?

Vanessa looks like she's giving up hope. Then suddenly,

                              VANESSA (CONT'D)
                    Oh my God - It moved! I felt it!

                              JUNO
                         (nods)
                    Elbow.

                              VANESSA
                    Wow! It's magical.

Juno smiles at Vanessa in awe of her genuine affection.

85   EXT. SUBURBAN STREETS - MORNING   85

The streets are covered in muddy, slushy snow. The mud is
instantly TRAMPLED underfoot by the collective feet of the
Dancing Elk Track Team on their morning run.

85A   INT. MACGUFF HOUSE - BREN'S DESK - DAY   85A

Bren cuts the top three inches off a pair of Juno's jeans.
Then, using a sewing machine, begins attaching an elastic
waistband.

85B   INT. DANCING ELK SCHOOL - CORRIDOR - DAY   85B

We're behind that same WAISTBAND, as Juno walks through the
students. Now, people seem to part the waters for the belly.

85C   INT. LORING HOUSE - MARK'S "SPECIAL ROOM" - DAY   85C

Mark has the Les Paul on his lap as he stares at the boards
of an awful commercial.

CU - THE SCRIPT (storyboards). A kitchen scene with a kid
eating a new breakfast product called - BRUNCH BOWLZ.

Annoyed and out of ideas, Mark begins an impromptu song...

                    MARK
          IF YOU'RE TIRED OF BREAKFAST BUT
          NOT HUNGRY FOR LUNCH, MICROWAVE
          YOURSELF A HEALTHY BOWL OF BRUNCH!

Mark drops his head, dejected. Then, the phone rings.

                    MARK
               (picks up)
          Hello?

INTERCUT WITH:

85D   INT. DANCING ELK SCHOOL - PHONE BOOTH - DAY   85D

                    JUNO
          So, I've been spending a lot of
          time listening to that weird CD you
          made me.

Mark instantly smiles.

                    MARK
          Oh really? What's the verdict?

                    JUNO
          I sort of like it. I mean, it's
          cute.

                    MARK
          Cute?

                    JUNO
          Well, when you're used to the raw
          power of Iggy and the Stooges,
          everything else sounds kind of
          precious by comparison.

                    MARK
          I imagine you have a collection of
          punk chestnuts to prove your point.

                                        (CONTINUED)

85D   CONTINUED: 85D

                              JUNO
                    Consider it your musical education.

                              MARK
                    I'm dying to see what you've got to
                    teach me.

                              JUNO
                    Okay, stop surfing porn and get
                    back to work. Just wanted to say
                    hi.

                              MARK
                    Go learn something.

          Mark hangs up. Smiles.

86   INT. DANCING ELK SCHOOL - CAFETERIA - DAY   86

          CU on Juno's tray sliding along, picking up an odd combo of
          pregnant food.

          Pull up to find Juno and Leah walking their trays to a table.

                              LEAH
                    God, you're getting huge. How many
                    months has it been now?

                              JUNO
                    Almost eight. You wouldn't believe
                    how weird I look naked.

                              LEAH
                    I wish my funbags would get bigger.

                              JUNO
                    Trust me, you don't. I actually
                    have to wear a bra now. And I have
                    to rub this nasty cocoa butter
                    stuff all over myself or my skin
                    could get stretched too far and
                    explode.

                              LEAH
                    Hot!

86A   INT. DANCING ELK SCHOOL - CORRIDOR - DAY   86A

          Juno and Leah are sitting inside an emptied awards case on
          the wall, eating their lunch.

                                                        (CONTINUED)

Juno notices that the other kids in the cafeteria can't help but glance her way. Some look derisive, others are amused.

                    JUNO
          God, why is everyone always staring
          at me?

                    LEAH
          Well, you are kind of...convex.

She illustrates by making a rounded gesture near her stomach.

                    JUNO
          Wow, someone's been actually doing
          her geometry homework for once!

                    LEAH
          I don't have a choice. Keith's been
          grading me really hard lately.

                    JUNO
          Please do not refer to Mr. Conyers
          as "Keith," okay? My barf reflex is
          already heightened these days.

                    LEAH
          Keith's hot.

                    JUNO
          Eww, he's all *beardy!*

We see KEITH the teacher talking to some science kids in the background. He has a *Wild America* beard. He lifts a cup of coffee to his lips and slurps lustily.

Back on Juno and Leah:

                    LEAH
          Did you hear Bleek is going to prom
          with Katrina De Voort?

                    JUNO
          Katrina? Pfft, no way. He doesn't
          like Katrina. It must be a pity date.

                    LEAH
               (shrugging)
          He asked her. I heard they were
          going to Benihana, then the prom,
          then to Vijay's parents' cabin.

                                              (CONTINUED)

> JUNO
> Bleeker told me Katrina's whole
> house reeks of soup!

> LEAH
> Oh, it totally does. I was there
> for her birthday about four years
> ago and it was like Lipton Landing.
> But you know, boys have endured
> worse things for nookie.

> JUNO
> There's no way in hell they're
> having sex or even holding hands.

> LEAH
> I wouldn't be so sure about that.
> He did it with you. He's a man now.

> JUNO
> Yeah, well, Bleek trusted me. We're
> best friends.

> LEAH
> Are you jealous? I thought you said
> you didn't care what he did.

> JUNO
> I'm not jealous, and I don't care.
> I just know he doesn't like Katrina
> and I don't think he should toy
> with her emotions like that. She
> seems so nice and all.

> LEAH
> Okay Juno, I'm really convinced.

> JUNO
> Prom is for wenises, anyway. Once
> you're old enough to go, it's not
> cool anymore.

87   INT. DANCING ELK SCHOOL - BLEEKER'S LOCKER - DAY   87

Bleeker retrieves a book from his open locker. Juno marches
up to him, belly leading the way.

> JUNO
> Are you honestly and truly going to
> prom with Katrina De Voort?

                              BLEEKER
                    Um, hi?

                              JUNO
                    Leah just told me you were going
                    with her.

                              BLEEKER
                    Yeah, I did ask her if she wanted
                    to go. A bunch of us from the team
                    are going to Benihana, then the
                    prom, then Vijay's parents' cabin.

Juno is clearly AFFRONTED.

                              BLEEKER
                         (meekly)
                    We're getting a stretch limo.

                              JUNO
                    Your mom must be really glad you're
                    not taking me.

                              BLEEKER
                    You're mad. Why are you mad?

                              JUNO
                    I'm not mad. I'm in a fucking great
                    mood. Despite the fact that I'm
                    trapped in a fat suit I can't take
                    off, despite the fact that everyone
                    is making fun of me behind my back,
                    despite the fact that *your* little
                    girlfriend gave me the stinkeye in
                    art class yesterday...

                              BLEEKER
                    Katrina's not my girlfriend! And I
                    doubt she was actually giving you
                    the stinkeye. She just looks like
                    that all the time.

A GIRL strides past (obviously KATRINA) with a sour look
aimed squarely at Juno.

                              JUNO
                    Whatever. Have fun at the prom with
                    Soupy Sales. I'm sure I can think
                    of something way more cool to do
                    that night.
                         (MORE)

                    JUNO (cont'd)
          Like I could pumice my feet, or go
          to Bren's dumb Unitarian church, or
          get hit by a ten-ton truck full of
          hot garbage juice. All those things
          would be exponentially cooler than
          going to the prom with you.

She starts to walk away.

Bleeker takes a deep breath.

                    BLEEKER
          You're being really immature.

                    JUNO
               (turning around)
          What?

Bleeker BRACES himself and pushes up his lab goggles.

                    JUNO
          That's not how our thing works! I
          hurl the accusations and you talk
          me down, remember?

                    BLEEKER
          Not this time. You don't have any
          reason to be mad at me. You broke
          my heart. I should be royally
          ticked at you, man. I should be
          really cheesed off. I shouldn't
          want to talk to you anymore.

                    JUNO
          Why? Because I got bored and had
          sex with you one day, and then I
          didn't, like, *marry* you?

                    BLEEKER
          Like I'd marry you! You would be the
          meanest wife of all time. And anyway,
          I know you weren't bored that day
          because there was a lot of stuff on
          TV. *The Blair Witch Project* was on
          Starz, and you were like, "Oh, I want
          to watch this, but we should make out
          instead. La la la."

                    JUNO
          Forget it, Bleek. Take Katrina the
          Douche Packer to the prom. I'm sure
          you guys will have a really
          bitchin' time!

                                        (CONTINUED)

                              BLEEKER
                    (searching for a comeback)
                    Yeah, well...I still have your
                    underwear.

                              JUNO
                    I still have your virginity!

                              BLEEKER
                    (looking around, panicked)
                    Oh my God, SHUT UP!

                              JUNO
                    What? Are you ashamed that we did it?

                              BLEEKER
                    No...

                              JUNO
                    Well at least you don't have to
                    walk around with the evidence under
                    your sweater. I'm a planet!

Juno picks up her BACKPACK dejectedly and slides it over her
shoulder. She's about to walk away, when...

                              BLEEKER
                    Wait, let me take that.

                              JUNO
                    Huh?

                              BLEEKER
                    You shouldn't be carrying that
                    heavy bag. I'll take it.

                              JUNO
                    Oh. It's fine. What's another ten
                    pounds?

She turns around, wipes TEARS off her cheek (making sure no
one sees) and continues down the hallway.

87   OMITTED   88

88A   OMITTED   88A

89   EXT. MACGUFF HOUSE - PREVIA - DAY   89

Juno climbs ungracefully into the van. She starts the engine,
then pauses to dig through her backpack for something. She
produces a brush and begins brushing her hair in the rearview
mirror, examining herself self-consciously. She puts on some
Dr. Pepper Lip Smacker and backs out of the driveway.

90   INT. LORING HOUSE - MARK'S SPECIAL ROOM - DAY   90

Mark is seated at the computer, surfing a horror movie
website. He has the blank expression of a bored obsessive.
The doorbell rings.

91   INT. LORING HOUSE - ENTRY - DAY   91

Mark opens the door. Juno stands there, looking radiantly
knocked-up. She holds a stack of CDs. Mark breaks into a
grin.

                         MARK
                Wow. That shirt is working hard.

                         JUNO
                    (furtive)
                Is Vanessa here?

                         MARK
                Nope. We're safe.

He and Juno smile conspiratorially.

                         JUNO
                Cool.

                         MARK
                Come on, I have something for you.

He gestures for Juno to follow him into the house.

92   INT. LORING HOUSE - BASEMENT - AFTERNOON   92

The Lorings' basement is dank, cluttered unfinished and
unattractive, much like Paulie Bleeker's. Mark pulls a chain
to illuminate a bare bulb.

                                                    (CONTINUED)

> JUNO
> Oh, Mark! Is this the baby's room?
> It's beautiful!

> MARK
> Hilarious. No, I just keep all of
> my old comics down here, and I want
> to show you one of them.

> JUNO
> Oh God, you're one of *those* guys...

> MARK
> You're gonna like this, I promise.

Mark RUMMAGES through a cardboard box in the corner.

> MARK
> (extracting a bagged COMIC
> from the box)
> Here it is.

He shows the COMIC to Juno. It's called "Most Fruitful Yuki." It
depicts a pregnant JAPANESE GIRL kicking ass and taking names.

> JUNO
> "Most Fruitful Yuki"? What is...Oh
> my god, she's a pregnant superhero!

> MARK
> Isn't that great? I got it when I
> was in Japan with my band. She
> reminds me of you.

Juno examines the comic. "Most Fruitful Yuki" does resemble her.

> JUNO
> Wow, I actually feel like less of a
> fat dork now.

> MARK
> Most Fruitful Yuki is bad ass, man.
> You should be proud to be the same
> condition.

She throws a KARATE KICK in Mark's direction with a KEE-YA!

Juno is sincerely pleased.

> JUNO
> Okay, how about some tunes?

There's a battered portable CD player in the corner. Juno
kneels down and pops in one of the discs.

                    JUNO
          Now this first one is kinda slow.
          But it's Mott the Hoople so it's
          still totally rad and hardcore.

Juno puts in the CD and "All The Young Dudes" fills the room.

Mark Laughs.

                    JUNO
          What?

                    MARK
          I actually know this one.

                    JUNO
          You do?

                    MARK
          Yeah, this song's older than me, if
          you can believe that. I danced to
          it at my senior prom.

                    JUNO
          That's almost interesting, Mark.
          Who did you dance with?

                    MARK
          Her name was Cynthia Vogel and she
          was a good dance partner. Even let
          me put my hands on her butt.

                    JUNO
          Oh man, I can just picture you slow
          dancing like a dork!

She mockingly places her hands on Mark's waist and moves back
and forth stiffly.

                    MARK
          No, I put my hands on your waist.
          Then you put your arms around my
          neck. That's how we did it in '88.

Mark puts his hands on what remains of Juno's waist. She
drapes her arms around his neck self-consciously.

                    JUNO
          Oh, okay. Like this.

                                              (CONTINUED)

                    MARK
          You've never been to a dance, have
          you?

                    JUNO
               (casually defensive)
          Only squares and nerds go to dances.

                    MARK
          What are you?

                    JUNO
          I don't know.

They SWAY slowly to the music. Juno's belly bumps up against
Mark.

                    MARK
          I feel like there's something
          between us.

They laugh.

Juno rests her head on Mark's chest. They dance in silence
for a few moments, then stop moving. Mark pulls Juno as close
as he possibly can, given her expanding girth.

                    MARK
          I'm leaving Vanessa.

                    JUNO
               (quiet at first)
          What?

                    MARK
          It's just not working out, but I'm
          getting my own place in the city...
          and I've got it all planned out.
          It's something I've wanted to do
          for a long time...

Juno backs away.

                    JUNO
               (growing)
          No.

                    MARK
          No?

                    JUNO
          No. No, you definitely cannot do
          that, Mark. That's a big, fat sack
          of *no*!

                    MARK
          What's the matter?

                    JUNO
          This isn't what we agreed on. You
          guys have to take care of...this!
          You are the chosen custodians of
          the big-ass bump!

She GESTURES wildly to her belly. Suddenly, something matters
to her far more than the approval of an older guy.

                    MARK
          But I thought you'd be cool if...

                    JUNO
              (interrupting)
          I want <u>you</u> guys to adopt the
          Buglet. I wanted everything to be
          perfect. Not shitty and broken like
          everyone else's family. Listen,
          once I have the baby, Vanessa is
          going to finally be happy, and
          everything will be all right.
          Believe me on this one!

                    MARK
          A baby is not going to fix
          everything. Besides, I don't know if
          I'm ready to be a father.

                    JUNO
              (aghast)
          But you're *old!*

                    MARK
          I...How do you think of me, Juno?
          Why are you here?

                    JUNO
          I don't know. I just liked being your
          friend. I sort of liked becoming
          furniture in your weird life.

                    MARK
          This...
              (he gestures to the dank
               surrounding room)
                    (MORE)

                                        (CONTINUED)

                    MARK (cont'd)
          ...this is what my life has become.
          Stuff in boxes. Stuff underground.
          Is that so appealing to you?

                    JUNO
          Yeah, I guess...Is this my fault? Is
          Vanessa mad at you because of me?

                    MARK
          That's not the point. We're just
          not in love anymore.

                    JUNO
          Yeah, but didn't you love Vanessa
          when you married her? If you love
          someone once, you can love them
          again, I know it. My friend Leah has
          gone out with the same guy, like,
          four times. You're just not trying.

Mark suddenly sees Juno for what she is - a teenage girl.

                    MARK
          I'm such an idiot. I can't believe
          what an idiot I am.

He paces over to the wall and KICKS it softly.

                    JUNO
          Please don't get a divorce! God,
          Mark, just do me a solid and stay
          with your wife.

                    MARK
          God, you're so young.

                    JUNO
          Not really. I'm sixteen. I'm old
          enough to tell when people are
          acting like total a-holes!

Juno turns to leave, then shoots one furious look back at
Mark.

                    JUNO
          Oh and by the way, I bought another
          Sonic Youth album and it's the
          worst thing I've ever heard! It's
          just *noise,* man!

She bolts up the stairs, sobbing.

STILLS

93   INT. LORING HOUSE - LIVING ROOM - DAY   93

Juno reaches the top of the stairs and scrambles toward the
front door, only to be intercepted by Vanessa, who's
returning home from work, carrying her briefcase and a
freshly purchased NURSING PILLOW. They nearly collide.

                    VANESSA
          Juno? What's going on?

                    JUNO
     Nothing.

It's obvious from Juno's tears and flushed face that she's
lying. Vanessa instantly goes pale with fear, but she tries
her hardest to seem serene and "together" in front of Juno.

                    VANESSA
               (pretending to be calm)
          Mark? Why is Juno crying?

                    JUNO
          I'm not crying. I'm allergic to
          fine home furnishings. See you
          later.

She rushes toward the door.

                    VANESSA
          Hold on.

Juno halts.

                    VANESSA
          Juno, what's the matter?

                    MARK
          She's hormonal. Right, June? It's
          just part of the whole process.

Juno looks totally betrayed. She doesn't respond. Vanessa
looks at Juno's expression and knows Mark is lying.

                    VANESSA
          What did you do?

                    MARK
          I didn't do anything... I just...
          I've just been thinking.

The worst words a man can speak.

(CONTINUED)

> VANESSA
> (*you've been thinking?*)
> What?

> MARK (CONT'D)
> Just thinking if this is really the
> right thing for us.

> VANESSA
> What are you referring to?

She knows exactly to what he's referring.

> MARK
> I've been just wondering if we're,
> you know, ready.

> VANESSA
> Of course we're ready. We've taken
> all the classes. The nursery. The
> books -

> MARK
> I know we're prepared. I just don't
> know if... I'm ready.

Juno's face continues to fall. Vanessa notices.

> VANESSA
> (to Juno)
> Juno, don't worry about this. He just
> has cold feet. That's how boys are.
> The books all say the same thing. A
> woman becomes a mother when she gets
> pregnant. A man becomes a father when
> he sees his baby. He's going to get
> there. He'll get there.

Juno ain't buying it.

> VANESSA (CONT'D)
> (to Mark)
> Why don't we let Juno go home and we
> can discuss this later on, okay?

> MARK
> It all just happened so fast. We
> put that ad in the paper. I thought
> it would take months if, you know,
> ever and then - boom - Two weeks
> later, she's in our living room.

                        VANESSA
                    (quietly)
                She answered our prayers.

                        MARK
                    (ignores the comment)
                Ever since, it's just been like a
                ticking clock.

This stops Vanessa. Juno looks offended.

                        VANESSA
                What are you saying?

A long hideous beat.

                        MARK
                It just feels a little like bad
                timing.

Another hideous beat.

                        VANESSA
                What would be a good time for you?

                        MARK
                I don't know. There's just things I
                still want to do.

                        VANESSA
                Like what? Be a rock star?

                        MARK
                Don't mock me.

Vanessa sighs. It's done.

                        VANESSA
                You're trying to do something that's
                never going to happen. And you know
                what? Your shirt is stupid. Grow up.
                If I have to wait for you to become
                Kurt Cobain, I'm never going to be a
                mother.

Vanessa looks defeated.

                        MARK (CONT'D)
                I never said I'd be a great father.

We hear the front door closing. Vanessa and Mark look over
and notice that Juno has escaped the conflict.

94   EXT. LORING HOUSE - AFTERNOON   94

Juno runs up to her car sobbing. She struggles with the keys, but finally makes it into the Previa and drives off.

EXT. HIGHWAY - AFTERNOON

The Previa slides off the road and comes to a stop on the shoulder.

INT. PREVIA - AFTERNOON

Juno buckles over the steering wheel, crying, unwinding for the first time since she became pregnant.

After a beat, she begins to gather herself.

INT. BLEEKER'S BEDROOM - NIGHT

Bleeker is sitting next to his bed, noodling on the guitar. He's playing a theme that we will soon recognise.

EXT. CORNER STORE - NIGHT

Juno lays on the hood of her Previa, contemplating her future. We push in close... when she gets an idea.

She hops off the hood and scurries into the Previa where she finds a crumpled up Jiffy Lube receipt. She unfolds it and pulls out a pen, ready to write something... a note?

EXT. LORING HOUSE - NIGHT

It's quiet after the storm. Inside, we see Vanessa sitting alone at her perfect dining room table, drinking a glass of wine.

103   INT. LORING HOUSE - DINING ROOM - NIGHT   103

Vanessa takes a sip and continues to let the days events sink in. After a beat, Mark comes down the stairs to join her.

                         MARK
              I called Gerta Rauss. She says she
              can represent both of us. They call
              it "collaborative divorce." It's
              apparently all the rage right now.
                         (MORE)

                                              (CONTINUED)

CONTINUED:

                    MARK (cont'd)
          And it's easy because we don't have
          children.

                    VANESSA
          No, it's fine. Thanks for making
          the call, I guess.

Mark nods and sits down.

                    VANESSA
          We're actually, finally doing this?

                    MARK
          Looks like it, yeah.

                    VANESSA
          Have you found a place to stay?

                    MARK
          Yeah, downtown.

                    VANESSA
          A hotel?

                    MARK
          It's a loft.

                    VANESSA
              (lightly teasing)
          Aren't you the cool guy?

They STARE at the wall, speechless and defeated.

                    VANESSA
          I wanted a baby so bad. So bad.

She buries her head in her hands.

                    MARK
          I know you did.

There's a LOUD KNOCK on the front door.

EXT. LORING HOUSE - ENTRY - NIGHT

Mark opens the door. There's a folded piece of paper sitting
on the doormat. He squints and sees Juno pulling away in the
van.

Mark carefully unfolds the piece of paper--it takes a minute
because of Juno's proficiency in "teen girl origami." He
holds it up. We can see there's WRITING on the back.

                                              (CONTINUED)

CONTINUED:

> MARK
> It looks like a bill from Jiffy-
> Lube.

Vanessa takes the note from his hand and turns it over, examining it.

> VANESSA
> It's for me.

95   EXT. MACGUFF HOUSE - NIGHT   95

Juno parks her car and walks up to her house. A porch light's been left on for her, and the place looks cozy and inviting.

> JUNO V.O.
> I never realize how much I like being
> home unless I've been somewhere
> really different for a while.

She picks a CROCUS from the unkempt garden near the porch and sniffs it. She lifts her shirt and tickles her belly with it. Then she tucks the flower into her unkempt hair.

96   INT. MACGUFF HOUSE - KITCHEN - NIGHT   96

Mac is alone at the kitchen table going over the family finances while drinking one of Bren's weight loss shakes.

Juno enters.

> JUNO
> Hi Dad.

> MAC
> Hey, big puffy version of Junebug.
> Where have you been?

> JUNO
> Dealing with stuff way beyond my
> maturity level. Where is everyone?

> MAC
> Bren took Liberty Bell to her tot
> ice skating class.

> JUNO
> Tot ice skating? Tots can't ice
> skate. Liberty Bell's still getting
> the hang of stairs.

(CONTINUED)

                          MAC
          No, but you know Bren. She dreams big.

                          JUNO
          Yeah, she does.

                          MAC
          You look a little morose, honey.
          What's eating you?

                          JUNO
          I'm losing my faith in humanity.

                          MAC
          Think you can narrow it down for me.

                          JUNO
          I guess I wonder sometimes if
          people ever stay together for good.

                          MAC
          You mean like couples?

                          JUNO
          Yeah, like people in love.

                          MAC
          Are you having boy trouble? I gotta be
          honest; I don't much approve of you
          dating in your condition, 'cause... well,
          that's kind of messed up.

                          JUNO
          Dad, no!

                          MAC
          Well, it's kind of skanky. Isn't
          that what you girls call it?
          Skanky? Skeevy?

                          JUNO
          Please stop now.

                          MAC
               (persisting)
          Tore up from the floor up?

                          JUNO
          Dad, it's not about that. I just need
          to know that it's possible for two
          people to stay happy together
          forever. Or at least for a few years.

                                                    (CONTINUED)

                    MAC
It's not easy, that's for sure.
Now, I may not have the best track
record in the world, but I have
been with your stepmother for ten
years now, and I'm proud to say
that we're very happy.

Juno nods in agreement.

                    MAC (CONT'D)
In my opinion, the best thing you
can do is to find a person who
loves you for exactly what you are.
Good mood, bad mood, ugly, pretty,
handsome, what have you, the right
person will still think that the
sun shines out your ass. That's the
kind of person that's worth
sticking with.

A wave of REALIZATION crosses Juno's face.

                    JUNO
I sort of already have.

                    MAC
Well, of course. Your old D-A-D!
You know I'll always be there to
love and support you, no matter
what kind of pickle you're in.

He nods toward her belly.

                    MAC
Obviously.

Juno laughs and hugs her father, planting a smooch on his
cheek.

                    JUNO
I need to go out somewhere for just
a little while. I don't have any
homework, and I swear I'll be back
by ten.

She salutes and dashes out of the kitchen.

                    MAC
You *were* talking about me, right?

Montage:

96A   OMITTED   96A

97   OMITTED   97

98   OMITTED   98

99   OMITTED   99

100   INT. BLEEKER HOUSE - BLEEKER'S ROOM - NIGHT   100

We push in over Bleeker sleeping in his car-bed towards the
window. We look out onto the lawn to find Juno and Leah
running back to the Previa, hopping in, and screeching off.

100A   OMITTED   100A

100B   OMITTED   100B

100C   OMITTED   100C

100D   OMITTED   100D

101   EXT. BLEEKER HOUSE - MORNING   101

Bleeker steps out of the house for his usual early-morning run.

He looks down to see a message scrawled in chalk on the
stoop: "BLEEKER- CHECK THE MAIL."

He walks down to the end of the driveway and opens the latch
on the mailbox.

At *least* one hundred containers of ORANGE TIC TACS come pouring
out in an colorful deluge. They spill out onto the driveway.

Bleeker smiles.

102   EXT. DANCING ELK SCHOOL - TRACK - MORNING   102

Juno waddles toward the field. The guys on the track team,
ridiculously arrayed as usual, are doing hurdler stretches.
They stare at her quizzically. Bleeker spots Juno approaching
and jogs up to the chainlink fence.

                                                  (CONTINUED)

                              BLEEKER
            Did you put like a hundred things
            of Tic Tacs in my mailbox?

                              JUNO
            Yeah. That was me.

                              BLEEKER
            Why?

                              JUNO
                 (blushes)
            Because they're your fave. And you
            can never have too much of your
            favorite one-calorie breath mint.

                              BLEEKER
            Well...thanks. I think I'm pretty
            much set until college on the Tic
            Tac front.

                              JUNO
            You know, I've been thinking. I'm
            really sorry I was such a huge
            bitch to you. You didn't deserve
            that. You never deserve any of the
            poo I unload on you.

                              BLEEKER
            You know it's okay.

                              JUNO
            Also, I think I'm in love with you.

                              BLEEKER
            What, you mean as friends?

                              JUNO
            No, for real. I think you are the
            coolest person I've ever met. And
            you don't even have to try.

                              BLEEKER
            I try really hard, actually...

                              JUNO
            No, you're naturally smart. You
            always think of the funniest things
            to do. Remember when you passed me
            that postcard during Spanish class,
            and it was addressed like, "Junebug
            MacGuff, Row 4, Third Seat From the
            Blackboard"?
                              (MORE)

                    JUNO (cont'd)
          And it said, "I'm having fun in
          Barcelona- wish you were here"?
          That was hilarious.

                    BLEEKER
          I was just bored. I only think school
          is awesome like, 80% of the time.

                    JUNO
          Plus, you're the only person who
          doesn't stare at my stomach all the
          fucking time. You actually look at my
          face. And every time I look at you,
          the baby starts kicking me super hard.

                    BLEEKER
          It does?

Juno presses Bleeker's hand against her belly.

                    BLEEKER
          Wizard!

                    JUNO
          I think it's because my heart
          starts pounding when I see you.

                    BLEEKER
          Mine too.

                    JUNO
          Basically, I'm completely smitten
          with you, and I don't care if I'm
          making an ass out of myself right
          now, because you've seen me make an
          ass out of myself a million times,
          and you still want to be my friend.

                    BLEEKER
          Well, yeah. You're the best friend
          I've ever had, even when you're
          being kind of evil.

                    JUNO
          That's all I need from you. That's
          more than I could ever ask for.
          You're just golden, dude.

                    BLEEKER
          Can we make out now?

                    JUNO
          Okay.

102   CONTINUED: (3)   102

Bleeker and Juno KISS, oblivious to the gawking track team
guys in the background.

In the distance, near the school entrance, we see STEVE
RENDAZO (the kid who always TORMENTS Juno) regarding the
makeout session with a sad, envious expression.

LEAH passes by, does a double take, then hurries up to the
fence, rolling her eyes.

                        LEAH
                    (disgusted)
            You know, you can go into early
            labor sucking face like that!

Juno gives her the FINGER, not breaking the clinch with Bleeker.

105   INT. MACGUFF HOUSE - JUNO'S BEDROOM - MORNING   105

Juno is lying on her back on the bed, staring at the ceiling.
She's more pregnant than we've ever seen her. She revs a
Matchbox car against the slope of her belly and lets it roll.

Juno suddenly sits up, looking thoroughly freaked. She pats
her lap frantically and jumps off the bed.

                        JUNO
            Dad!

INTERCUT WITH:

105A   INT. MACGUFF HOUSE - MAC'S WORK DESK - SAME   105A

Mac looks up from the lure he's working on.

                        MAC (O.C.)
            What?!

                        JUNO
            Either I just pissed my pants or...

                        MAC (O.C.)
            Or...

                        JUNO
            Thundercats are go!

106   EXT. MACGUFF HOUSE - DAY   106

Mac, Bren and Liberty Bell rush out of the house. They pile
into the Previa at breakneck speed. Juno waddles behind them,
protesting.

107   INT. HOSPITAL - DAY   107

CU of Juno wearing a puffy surgical cap. She's being pushed
down the hospital corridor in a wheelchair. She bursts into
giggles. Pull back to reveal her that Leah is pushing her
rather aggressively. Leah jokingly steers the wheelchair into
a wall. Juno feigns whiplash.

Bren appears behind them and orders Juno out of the
wheelchair, exasperated. She pulls off Juno's surgical cap.
Leah and Juno snicker.

108   INT. HOSPITAL - BIRTHING SUITE - DAY   108

We see Juno is in a BIRTHING SUITE at the hospital, pacing
impatiently, bent over in obvious discomfort. She's wearing
her Chuck Taylors and knee socks with her hospital gown. Leah
and Bren stand nearby.

Juno doubles over in pain.

                    JUNO
                (panicked)
          Ow, ow, fuckity-ow. Bren, when do I
          get that Spinal Tap thing?

                    BREN
          It's called a spinal *block*, and you
          can't have it yet, honey. The doctor
          said you're not dilated enough.

                    JUNO
          You mean I have to wait for it to
          get even worse? Why can't they just
          give it to me now?

                    BREN
          Well, honey, doctors are sadists
          who like to play God and watch
          lesser people scream.

Juno lets out a genuine shriek of pain.

                                                        (CONTINUED)

108   CONTINUED: 108

                          BREN
                    (checking her watch)
              Shit.
                    (To the doctor)
              Hey, can we give my kid the damn
              spinal tap already?

109   INT. HOSPITAL - BIRTHING SUITE - LATER   109

                          JUNO V.O.
              It really didn't hurt that bad
              having him.

       We see Juno in the process of delivery, from her POV. Leah
       holds one of Juno's feet and Bren holds the other.

                          JUNO V.O.
              The best part was when I peed on
              Leah during labor.

       We see Leah holding Juno's FOOT, which is shaking. Leah's
       shirt is soaked. She rolls her eyes and mouths "Fuck you" at
       Juno. Juno's raised MIDDLE FINGER enters the frame.

                          JUNO V.O.
              And then, out of nowhere, there
              it was...

       The doctor reveals JUNO'S BABY BOY above the sheet.

                          JUNO (V.O.)
              There he was.

       Juno looks at the baby in awe, then her eyes begin to
       flutter... and she passes out.

110   EXT. DANCING ELK SCHOOL - TRACK - AFTERNOON   110

       Paulie Bleeker is running as fast as his legs can carry him
       on the Dancing Elk track. There's a very sparse crowd in the
       bleachers. As Paulie approaches the tape, his envious
       teammate Vijay looks on. Bleeker's mom is seated near Vijay,
       holding a video camera.

                          JUNO V.O.
              I decided to not call Bleeker to
              tell him that I was having the
              baby. He had a big meet against
              Manteno and I didn't want him to
              get all worried about me and choke.

                                                           (CONTINUED)

110   CONTINUED: 110

Paulie breaks the tape, winning the race. The fifteen or so
people in attendance cheer.

                    VIJAY
               (admiringly)
          His legs are as swift as his seed.

                    MRS. BLEEKER
          What did you say?

Bleeker pants at the finish line, dripping with sweat.

                    ANNOUNCER
          P. Bleeker has just broken a
          district record in the 400.

Bleeker looks out at the BLEACHERS, scanning them for Juno.
She's not there.

                    JUNO V.O.
          But he figured it out anyway.

Bleek takes off RUNNING toward the parking lot without
stopping to explain. His mother stands up, confused.

111   INT. HOSPITAL - MATERNITY WARD - DAY   111

A NURSE reaches into one of the maternity ward bassinets and
gently lifts up a swaddled newborn baby.

The nurse turns and addresses an unseen spectator.

                    NURSE
          Would you like to meet your son?

Pull back to reveal she's speaking to VANESSA, who stands,
paralyzed, several feet away.

                    VANESSA
          I have a son?

                    NURSE
               (amused)
          You are the adoptive mother?

                    VANESSA
          I have a son.

                    NURSE
          Healthy kid, too. Didn't waste any
          time getting out.

                                                          (CONTINUED)

111   CONTINUED: 111

Vanessa reaches out for the baby and gingerly accepts him in
her eyes. She spends a few moments just looking at him.

She feels someone watching her, then looks up to see a Bren
leaning against the doorway.

Vanessa blinks away her tears self-consciously.

                    VANESSA
          How do I look?

                    BREN
               (gently)
          Like a mom. Scared shitless.

Vanessa laughs.

112   INT. HOSPITAL - BIRTHING SUITE - DAY   112

Juno is curled up on her bed in the birthing room. The birth
is obviously over; there's that air of stillness and
accomplishment, a task completed. The doctors have cleared
out. Mac sits in a chair next to the bed, looking like he's
not sure what to say.

He holds up a deck of Playing cards as if to initiate a game,
but Juno gently pushes his hand away. Their eyes meet. His
expression is helpless, hers is utterly drained.

                    MAC
          Someday, you'll be back here,
          honey. On your terms.

Juno nods and swallows.

Over Mac's shoulder, a silhouette appears in the doorway.
It's Bleeker in his track uniform.

Juno sees him and bursts into sudden, ragged sobs. Mac
glances at her, alarmed. Paulie moves toward the bed. Mac
clears his throat, gets up and leaves the room.

Paulie climbs onto the hospital bed and carefully puts his
arm around Juno. She leans into him, letting herself go for
the first time in months.

113   INT. HOSPITAL ROOM - BIRTHING SUITE - EVENING   113

Juno lies on the bed. She looks rested and relaxed compared
to her earlier crying jag, but her face is still pink and
swollen. Bleeker is curled up next to her, still in his track
uniform and spikes.

> JUNO V.O.
> Bleeker decided he didn't want to
> see the baby. Neither did I,
> really. He didn't feel like ours.

114   INT. HOSPITAL - MATERNITY WARD - EVENING   114

We see Vanessa leaning over the bassinet, unable to take her
eyes off the baby, touching it's hair reverently.

> JUNO V.O.
> I think he was always hers.

115   OMITTED   115

116   INT. LORING HOUSE - NURSERY - DAY   116

The nursery is perfectly decorated in Vanessa's immaculate
taste. Nothing looks as though it's been touched. We see the
antique ROCKING CHAIR sitting empty.

> JUNO V.O.
> It ended with a chair.

We pan past the wall Vanessa had said "needed something."
There's a framed note on the wall. It looks like it was
handwritten on the back of a Jiffy Lube bill. We see that it
says: "Vanessa - If you're still in, I'm still in. Juno."

We move to the door and get a view of Vanessa's bedroom. We
see her lying in bed with a burp cloth draped over her
shoulder, feeding the baby. For the first time ever, Vanessa
looks disorganized, unshowered--and incredibly happy. There
are formula bottles on the bedside table and a bassinet
pushed close to the bed. Obviously, she hasn't been away from
the baby for a single moment.

The baby reaches up and grabs Vanessa's thumb. Vanessa glows
with an expression of pure bliss.

117   OMITTED   117

118   OMITTED   118

119   EXT. MACGUFF HOUSE - DAY   119

It's a sparkling summer afternoon. Juno wheels her bicycle
out of the detached garage. She waves goodbye to Bren, who is
playing in the yard with two WEIMARANERS. She looks almost as
happy with her dogs as VANESSA looked with her baby.

120   EXT. SUBURBAN STREETS - DAY   120

Juno rides her bike aggressively down the street. Her guitar
is slung over her shoulder in a gig bag. She's obviously not
pregnant anymore. She looks happy, but older.

                    JUNO V.O.
          As boyfriends go, Paulie Bleeker is
          totally boss. He is the cheese to
          my macaroni. I know people are
          supposed to fall in love *before*
          they reproduce, but normalcy's not
          really our style.

As she tears recklessly down the street on her bikes, she
passes the Dancing Elk TRACK TEAM, still running in
outrageously skimpy shorts and bandanas.

Juno RIDES up to a garage where Bleeker is sitting, tuning
his guitar.

121   EXT. BLEEKER HOUSE - DAY   121

Juno bikes up to find Bleeker sitting on the stoop. She
smiles and takes out her guitar. She sits across from Bleeker
and pulls the pick out of the strings.

                    JUNO
          Ready?

Bleeker nods.

Juno begins strumming her guitar and playing "Anyone Else But
You," by the Moldy Peaches. Bleeker joins in. At first their
playing is discordant, but suddenly it works.

                    BLEEKER
          You're a part time lover and a full-
          time friend. The monkey on your
          back is the latest trend.
                    (MORE)

                    BLEEKER (cont'd)
          I don't see what anyone can see, in
          anyone else but you.

                    JUNO
          Here is the church and here is the
          steeple. We sure are cute for two
          ugly people. I don't see what anyone
          can see, in anyone else but you.

                    BLEEKER
          We both have shiny happy fits of
          rage. You want more fans, I want
          more stage. I don't see what anyone
          can see, in anyone else but you.

                    JUNO
          You are always trying to keep it
          real. I'm in love with how you
          feel. I don't see what anyone can
          see, in anyone else but you.

                    BLEEKER
          I kiss you on the brain in the shadow
          of a train. I kiss you all starry-
          eyed, my body's swinging from side to
          side. I don't see what anyone can
          see, in anyone else but you.

                    JUNO
          The pebbles forgive me, the trees
          forgive me. So why can't you
          forgive me? I don't see what anyone
          can see, in anyone else but you.

                    JUNO AND BLEEKER TOGETHER
          Du du du du du du dudu. Du du du du
          du du dudu. I don't see what anyone
          can see, in anyone else but you.

She and Bleeker exchange glances as they play. They smile
ambiguously. Juno leans over and kisses Bleeker on the cheek.

Pull out to reveal the surrounding green suburb buzzing with
life and summer activity.

                                        FADE TO BLACK

SOME COMMENTS ON *JUNO* BY SOME OF THE ACTORS

"Reading a Diablo Cody script is like going down a waterslide while eating an ice cream cone; it's cold and it gets your attention, and if some of it drips off of the cone onto your hands you can just rinse your hands off in the water underneath you."

—Michael Cera (Paulie Bleeker)

"Let me spew a few words at Diablo: When Jason Reitman hands you a script and says, 'Read this. This is GREAT,' the expectations are through the roof. When you read that script and it actually exceeds your ridiculous expectations... well, all you can do is hope you have a chance to be involved in bringing it to life. With a story and characters and dialogue this good, everyone involved in the making of the film has the same goal: Just don't screw it up. I think we didn't."

—J.K. Simmons (Mac MacGuff)

"I'm proud of this movie for what it's become, which is due entirely to Jason's eye and incredible spirit, and Ellen's ridiculous chops. Not to mention a cast of flawless performers and about a million other people, from those who conceptualized it to those who added its finishing touches. The way this film has moved from page to screen is nothing short of genius. I'm also proud merely to be associated with it, for it will surely go down in history as the famous, first-ever screenplay by the one and only Diablo Cody, to whom we all bow down.

"I remember little moments of filming, like sitting in a beat-up Previa next to Ellen Page, as we compared the intensity of the blue 'slurp 'n' swallow' slushie dye in our mouths. My hair was blonde, I was wearing a cardboard crown, and clad only in a fluorescent bra that was too big. The next scene, I found myself mutilating a mailbox with a baseball bat, drive-by style, while yelling obscenities about soup.

"All this was on my first night of filming. While neither of these scenes ended up in the final cut, they were certainly a fitting welcome to the job."

—Olivia Thirlby (Leah)

"Back in the day, when Diablo and I were strippers together, she told me about this little idea for a movie. I had no idea she would pop out a number like *Juno*—the funniest, smartest, most heartwarming look at a functioning dysfunctional American family I have ever read. I so badly wanted to be a part of this movie that I put my platform pumps and my tassels away. *Juno* makes me happy—thank you, Diablo."

—Jennifer Garner (Vanessa Loring)

CAST AND CREW CREDITS

FOX SEARCHLIGHT PICTURES Presents
A MANDATE PICTURES / MR. MUDD PRODUCTION
A JASON REITMAN FILM

"JUNO"

ELLEN PAGE MICHAEL CERA JENNIFER GARNER JASON BATEMAN ALLISON JANNEY
J.K. SIMMONS and OLIVIA THIRLBY

Casting by
MINDY MARIN, CSA
KARA LIPSON

Co-Producers
JIM MILLER
KELLI KONOP
BRAD VAN ARRAGON

Executive Producers
JOE DRAKE
NATHAN KAHANE
DANIEL DUBIECKI

Costume Designer
MONIQUE PRUDHOMME

Film Editor
DANA E. GLAUBERMAN

Produced by
LIANNE HALFON
JOHN MALKOVICH
MASON NOVICK
RUSSELL SMITH

Music by
MATEO MESSINA

Production Designer
STEVE SAKLAD

Songs by
KIMYA DAWSON

Director of Photography
ERIC STEELBERG

Written by
DIABLO CODY

Music Supervisors
PETER AFTERMAN and
MARGARET YEN

Directed by
JASON REITMAN

CAST

Juno MacGuff	Ellen Page
Paulie Bleeker	Michael Cera
Vanessa Loring	Jennifer Garner
Mark Loring	Jason Bateman
Bren MacGuff	Allison Janney
Mac MacGuff	J.K. Simmons
Leah	Olivia Thirlby
Gerta Rauss	Eileen Pedde
Rollo	Rainn Wilson
Steve Rendazo	Daniel Clark
Bleeker's Mom	Darla Vandenbossche
Vijay	Aman Johal
Su-Chin	Valerie Tian
Punk Receptionist	Emily Perkins
Ultrasound Technician . . .	Kaaren De Zilva
Guy Lab Partner .	Steven Christopher Parker
Girl Lab Partner	Candice Accola
Liberty Bell	Sierra Pitkin
Chemistry Teacher	Cut Chemist
Tough Girl	Eve Harlow
Nurse	Kirsten Williamson
Pretty-to-Goth Girl	Emily Tennant
Katrina De Voort	Ashley Whillans
Track Announcer	Jeff Witzke
Keith	Colin McSween
Sex Ed Teacher	Peggy Logan
RPG Nerd	Cameron Bright
Delivery Room Doctor	Joy Galmut
Vanessa's Friend #1	Wendy Russell
Vanessa's Friend #2	Robyn Ross
Dancing Elk Track Team . . .	Dallas Hanson
	Bryson Russell
	Derek Mann
	Keith Frost
	Grayson Grant
	Robin Watts
	Tyler Watts
	Brandon Barton
Stand-Ins	Katya Krotenko
	Kyle Reifsnyder
	Melissa Repka
	Saskia Gould

Stunt Coordinator . . . . Scott Ateah
Mandate Pictures Creative Executive
. . . . Mary Lee
Art Directors . . . . Michael Diner
Catherine Schroer
Art Department Coordinator . . . Lori West
Set Decorator . . . . Shane Vieau
Assistant Set Decorator . Melissa Grace Olson
Set Dressers . . . . . . Michael Jovanovski
Paul Hartman
Sergio Lavilla
Mike Church
Sigrid Spade
Christopher Wishart
Property Master . . . . . . Bryan Korenberg
Assistant Property Master . . . . Alex Cram
Camera Operator . . . . John Clothier
First Assistant Camera . . . Stewart Whelan
Second Assistant Camera . . . . Dean Morin
Second Assistant Camera . . . Patrick Houge
B-Camera First Assistant . . . . Dave Laurie
B-Camera Second Assistant . . . Ian Lavigne
Camera Loader . . . . Patrick Houge
Sound Mixer . . . . James Kusan
Boom Operator . . . . Tony Wyman
Sound Assistant . . . . Brad Kita
Key Makeup . . . . Victoria Down
Makeup . . . . Monica Huppert
Sandy Cooper
Makeup for J. Garner . . . . Ann Pala
Special Effects Makeup . . . . Lance Webb
Key Hair . . . . Sherry Gygli
Hair . . . . Robert Pandini
Assistant Costume Designer
. . . . Christine Coutts
Costumer for J. Garner . . . . Maria Bradley
Costume Set Supervisor . . . J. Paul Lavigne
Costumer . . . . Lise Hache
Truck Costumer . . . . Summer Eves
Production Accountant . . . . . Sue Levens
Assistant Accountants . . . Sydney LeClaire
Tania Rosa
Production Coordinator . Trevor Westerhoff
Assistant Production Coordinator
. . . . Sheryl Rhodes
2nd Assistant Production Coordinator
. . . . Jeff Wonnenberg
Clearance Coordinator . . . Peter Cummings
Second Assistant Directors . . . Josy Capkun
Gary Hawes
Third Assistant Director . . . . . Chad Belair
Script Supervisor . . . . Stephanie Rossel
Chief Lighting Technician . . . John Dekker

Assistant Chief Lighting Technician
. . . . Andrew Towsen
Lighting Technicians . . . . Randy Jablonka
Dave Leblanc
Rigging Chief Lighting Technician
. . . . Michael Mayo
Key Grip . . . . David Askey
Best Boy Grip . . . . Marty Coady
Dolly Grip . . . . David Kershaw
Grips . . . . Vince Phillips
Stephan Burianyk
Igor Bueller
Set Construction Coordinator . . John Beatty
Lead Carpenter . . . . . . Kevin Tomecek
Carpenter . . . . Dale Manzies
Paint Coordinator . . . . . . Doug Currie
Lead Painter . . . . Dusty Kelly
Key Greensperson . . . . Josi Bleuer
Greens . . . . D.J. Miller
Mike Carter
Johanna Manders
Location Manager . . . . Neil Robertson
Assistant Location Manager
. . . . Christian Thoma
Trainee Assistant Location Manager
. . . . Kris Kadzielski
Locations Coordinator . . . . . Keli Moore
Locations Scout . . . . Chris MacDonnell
Key Locations PA . . . . . . Holly Pinder
Production Assistants . . . . . Terry Wong
Corby Pinder
Dave Daniels
Alex Dias
Guitar Teachers . . . . Jason Faulkner
Hodges
Special Effects Supervisor . . . . John Sleep
Special Effects Technicians . . . Rory Cutler
Ken Reynolds
Mike Bolan
Ian Korver
Transportation Coordinator . . Clif Kosterman
Transport Captain . . . . . . Scott Delaplace
Transportation co-Captain . . Shawn O'Hearn
Security Coordinator . . . . Darren Pearson
Catering . . . . T.V. Dinners Ltd.
Chef . . . . Sandra Cinelli
Assistant Chefs . . . . . . Nicole Vaughan
Samantha Christian
First Aid/Craft Services . . . . Terri Willan
Ronda Simpson

POST PRODUCTION

Post Production Supervisor . . Jack Schuster
First Assistant Editor . . . . . Clay Rawlins
Post Production Assistant . . Omar Hassan-Reep

Editorial Intern . . . . . . Yanosh Cuglove
Music Editor. . . . . Nick South
Music Coordinator. . . . . . Alison Litton
Sound Editorial by . . . . . EarCandy, Inc.
Supervising Sound Editor . Perry Robertson
Supervising ADR Editor . . . Barney Cabral
Supervising Sound Designer/Re-Recording
    Mixer . . . . . . Scott Sanders, M.P.S.E.
Sound Editors. . Rickley W. Dumm, M.P.S.E.
                        Richard Dwan, Jr.
                        Fred Stahly, M.P.S.E.
First Assistant Sound Editor
. . . . Kevin A. Zimmerman
Foley Recorded at . . . . . . Post Creations
Foley Supervisor . . . . Nick Neutra
Foley Mixer . . . . Michael Kreple
Foley Artist . . . . Rick Owens
Re-Recording Mixers. . Ken S. Polk, C.A.S.
                J. Stanley Johnston, C.A.S.
Mix-Recordist. . . . . Gabe Serrano
ADR Mixer. . . . . Eric Thompson, C.A.S.
ADR Recordist . . . . Travis Mackay
Post Production Sound Services by
. . . . Wildfire Stages
Visual Effects by . . . . . Cos FX Films, Inc
Visual Effects Supervisor
. . . . Cosmas Paul Bolger, Jr.
Visual Effects Producer . . . . Sharon Stetzel
Visual Effects Production coordinator
. . . . Ken Locsmandi
CG Supervisor. . . . . . . Owen Holdren
CG Artists. . . . . Brandon Flyte
                        James Chu
                        Go Aoyama
Assistant to Mr. Reitman . . . Evan Godfrey
Assistant to Mr. Reitman and Mr. Dubiecki
. . . . Helen Estabrook
Assistant to Mr. Drake . . . . . . Soo Hugh
Assistant to Mr. Kahane . . Rachel Chapman
Assistant to Ms. Garner . . . . Emily Millard
Assistants to Mr. Mudd . Michael Stankevich
                        Shelley Dardon
Assistant to Mr. Novick . . . . . Matt Reis
Onset Assistants to the Producers
. . . . Lawra Robertson
                        Troy Sitter
                        Krista Kelloway
Vancouver Casting . . . . . . Coreen Mayrs
                        Heike Brandstatter
Unit Publicist . . . . Jeremy Walker
Still Photographer . . . . Doane Gregory
Dad Smile Photo. . . . . Jeff Witzke
Kid Smile Photos . . . . Josephine Reitman,
                Oliver Gorin, Ethan Steelberg

Ultrasound Baby . . . . . Matthew Sanders
Digital Intermediate by. . . . . . . EFILM
Colorist. . . . . Natasha Leonnet
Digital Intermediate Producer . . Loan Phan
Digital Intermediate Editor . . . Martha Pike
Digital Opticals . . . . Pat Clancey
Color Timing Assistant . . . . Tom Reiser
DI Consultant. . . . . Tim Krubsack
Main and End Titles by . Shadowplay Studio
Title Designers. . . . . Gareth Smith
                        Jenny Lee
Main Title Producer. . . Ari Sachter-Zeltzer
Negative Cutter . . . . . Executive Cutter
Laboratory and Transfer Services provided by
. . Technicolor Creative Services, Vancouver
Post Production services provided by
. . . . LA Digital Post
US production legal
. . . . Frankfurt Kurnit Klein & Selz
Canadian Production Legal . Karyn Edwards
Insurance Services . . . . . . Dewitt Stern

"Tire Swing," "My Rollercoaster,"
"So Nice So Smart,"
"I Like Giants," "Reminders of Then,"
"12/26," "Loose Lips"
Written and Performed by Kimya Dawson

"Tree Hugger," "Sleep"
Written by Kimya Dawson
Performed by Kimya Dawson and Antsy
Pants

"Once I Loved"
Written by Antonio Carlos Jobim, Vinicius
de Moraes, Ray Gilbert
Performed by Astrud Gilberto
Courtesy of The Verve Music Group
Under license from Universal Music
Enterprises

"All I Want Is You"
Written and Performed by Barry Louis
Polisar

"Besame Mucho"
Written by Consuelo Velazquez
Performed by Trio Los Panchos
Courtesy of SONY BMG Music
Entertainment (Mexico) S.A. de C.V.
By arrangement with SONY BMG MUSIC
ENTERTAINMENT

"A Well Respected Man"
Written by Ray Davies
Performed by The Kinks
Courtesy of Sanctuary Records

"Doll Parts"
Written by Courtney Love

"I'm Sticking With You"
Written by Lou Reed
Performed by The Velvet Underground
Courtesy of Universal Records
Under license from Universal Music
Enterprises

"Dearest"
Written by Bob Gibson, Ellas McDaniel,
Prentice Herman Polk, Jr.
Performed by Buddy Holly
Courtesy of Geffen Records
Under license from Universal Music
Enterprises

"Why Bother"
Written by Christopher McBride, Ryan
Parker, Chris Kemp, Sugar McGuinn
Performed by tHe drop
Courtesy of Loveless Records

"Superstar"
Written by Bonnie Bramlett, Delaney
Bramlett, Leon Russell
Performed by Sonic Youth
Courtesy of Geffen Records
Under license from Universal Music
Enterprises

"Piazza, New York Catcher"
Written by Sarah Martin, Stuart Murdoch,
Richard Colburn, Michael Cooke,
Christopher Geddes, Stephen Jackson, Bob
Kildea
Performed by Belle & Sebastian
Courtesy of Rough Trade Records Ltd.

"Expectations"
Written by Stuart Murdoch, Richard
Colburn, Michael Cooke, Christopher
Geddes, Stephen Jackson, Isobel Campbell
Performed by Belle & Sebastian
Courtesy of Jeepster Recordings and Matador
Records

"All The Young Dudes"
Written by David Bowie
Performed by Mott The Hoople
Courtesy of Columbia Records
By arrangement with SONY BMG MUSIC
ENTERTAINMENT

"Anyone Else But You"
Written by Adam Green, Kimya Dawson
Performed by The Moldy Peaches
Courtesy of Rough Trade Records Ltd.

"Sea of Love"
Written by Philip Baptiste, George Khoury
Performed by Cat Power
Courtesy of Matador Records

"Vampire"
Written by Leo Bear Creek
Performed by Antsy Pants

THE PRODUCERS WISH TO THANK
Eleanor O'Connor
The Bridge Studios
Nike
Gibson Guitars
The Marpole Curling Club
Sutton Place Hotel Vancouver
Ethan Berger
Melissa Havard
Angie Hensley
Kozyndan
David Choe
Tara McPherson
Rick Clark Productions
Creative Needle, Dallas
Eddie Lin
BC Film Commission
Minnesota Film Commission
The People of Vancouver, White Rock, and
Burnaby, British Columbia

MPAA # 43795

Prints by Deluxe

Panavision

Kodak

S.D.D.S.	Dolby	DTS
I.A.T.S.E.	Teamsters 155	UBCP

BIOS

Diablo Cody (Writer)

Diablo Cody penned her debut screenplay *Juno* while working as a phone sex operator/insurance adjuster in Minneapolis. She did not attend Harvard.

Cody has been featured in *Entertainment Weekly, Playboy, Elle*, and *Jane*, among other publications, and has appeared on CNN, the *FOX Morning Show*, and *Late Night with David Letterman*. In 2004, she authored the infamous and critically acclaimed memoir *Candy Girl: A Year in the Life of an Unlikely Stripper*. Most recently she wrote and co-created a half-hour series *The United States of Tara*, which will be executive produced by Steven Spielberg for Showtime. Cody is also working on her second book and various top-secret spec scripts.

Jason Reitman (Director)

Jason Reitman made his feature film directing debut with the 2006 hit *Thank You for Smoking*, based on the acclaimed 1994 novel by Christopher Buckley, which Reitman adapted for the screen. *Thank You for Smoking* had its world premiere at the 2005 Toronto Film Festival, where it was acquired by Fox Searchlight. The film went on to screen at the 2006 Sundance and SXSW Film Festivals, and Reitman was ultimately nominated for a Golden Globe award for Best Adapted Screenplay. In the wake of the success of *Thank You for Smoking*, Reitman and his producing partner, David Dubiecki, formed a new production company, Hard C, which is based at Fox Searchlight. Hard C is developing a number of projects, including the spec script "The Ornate Anatomy of Living Things."

Reitman was born in Montreal on October 19, 1977. He was on his first film set (*Animal House*) 11 days later. The son of director Ivan Reitman, he spent most of his childhood on or around film sets, surrounded by the funniest human beings on Earth. He even appeared in cameos in many of his father's films (*Twins, Ghostbusters II, Kindergarten Cop, Dave*, and *Father's Day*).

By 10, he was making the typical short films with his dad's home video camera. At 13, he got his first job on a film crew, as production assistant on *Kindergarten Cop*. At 15, Reitman made an AIDS public service announcement with actors from his high school that went on to win many awards and play on network television. Reitman graduated high school in 1995 and went on to USC to study English. There, he became a member of the comedy troupe Commedus

Interuptus and held a short stint as co-host of a morning radio show.

During his sophomore year in college, Reitman created a small collegiate desk calendar company that provided the budget for his first short film, *Operation*. The short comedy about kidney stealing went on to premiere at the 1998 Sundance Film Festival. At 19 years old, this made him one of the youngest directors ever to have a film at the festival.

This began a string of short films, including *H@* (premiered at South by Southwest 1999), *In God We Trust* (premiered at Sundance 2000, went on to play Toronto, Edinburgh, US Comedy Arts, New Directors/New Films at MoMa and won best short at many festivals, including Los Angeles, Aspen, Austin, Seattle, Florida, Athens, the New York Comedy Festival, and Bumbershoot Festival), *Gulp* (premiered at Sundance 2001), and *Consent* (premiered at Aspen Shorts Fest 2004 and won awards at Aspen and Seattle). Reitman's short films have played in over a hundred film festivals worldwide.

In early 2000, Reitman signed with the commercial production company Tate and Partners. In the five years since he began directing television advertising, he has received honors from the Cannes commercial awards, the Addys, as well as the highly coveted One Show. Selected clients include Heineken, Honda, Nintendo, BMW, Kyocera, Asics, Amstel Light, Baskin Robbins, GM, Burger King, and Denny's.

In beginning his professional career, Reitman fulfilled a lifelong dream by joining the Directors Guild of America; at that time he was the guild's second youngest member.